Shadows on the Wall:
Deterrence and Disarmament

Keith B. Payne

National Institute Press®

Published by
National Institute Press®
9302 Lee Highway, Suite 750
Fairfax, Virginia 22031

Library of Congress Cataloging-in-Publication Data

Names: Payne, Keith B., author.
Title: Shadows on the Wall : deterrence and disarmament / Keith B. Payne.
Other titles: Deterrence and disarmament
Description: Fairfax, Virginia : National Institute Press, [2020] |
    Summary: "Shadows on the Wall: Deterrence and Disarmament examines and
    contrasts the three alternative philosophical positions about the nature of the
    international system and patterns of human behavior that underlie three
    competing narratives seen in U.S. public debate regarding nuclear deterrence
    and disarmament. For over six decades, these three competing narratives, built
    on contrary philosophical traditions, have been the basis for contending
    positions regarding U.S. nuclear policy-ranging from advocacy for complete
    global nuclear disarmament to advocacy for the maintenance of robust U.S.
    nuclear capabilities for deterrence. Each of these three different narratives is
    based on different speculative expectations about developments in the
    international system and future patterns of human behavior. Given the
    inherent uncertainties about future developments in the international system
    and human behavior, none of these narratives can be deemed to objectively
    correct, or certainly wrong. They may, nevertheless, be judged to entail
    different levels of prudence for U.S. and allied security"-- Provided by
    publisher.
Identifiers: LCCN 2020004680 | ISBN 9780985555320 (paperback)
Subjects: LCSH: Deterrence (Strategy) | Nuclear arms control. | Nuclear
    disarmament. | Nuclear weapons--Government policy--United States.
Classification: LCC U162.6 .P395 2020 | DDC 355.02/17--dc23
LC record available at https://lccn.loc.gov/2020004680

For my wonderful growing family and in memory of Colin S. Gray, incomparable scholar, boss, mentor, colleague and friend.

Table of Contents

Foreword

Professor Keith Payne has written a bold analysis of our historical context that truly is a unique contribution to the American nuclear debate. His work here considers and describes most carefully what must be judged a global challenge to which there is no fully prudent solution. Russia is not going away anytime soon, though indeed already it is somewhat overshadowed by the large dragon to the East. In order to make sense clearly of what is happening, and why, Professor Payne makes admirable use of the familiar binary opposition of Realism and Idealism. He employs these for the keys they provide readily to help explain what otherwise typically is an unduly forbidding debate among experts.

For sensible-seeming reasons that we are able with high confidence to characterize as prudent tribalism, the three superpowers each behave competitively as players in our very own "Game of Thrones." What is most lacking, as Professor Payne argues very plausibly, is mutual trust. Indeed, it is the absence of trust, meaning confidence in essentially peaceable intentions, that is the most harmful of cultural elements globally. China, Russia, and yes, America too, do not trust each other to pursue goals, and choose ways harmless to the other superpowers. States compete in armament because, as political bodies responsible for the security of millions of people in a dangerous world, they simply have to do so; there is not an alternative, benign international political system on which they can plant their flag. To be blunt about it, the international political order just is what it is — an ultimately lawless "self-help" system. We cannot responsibly decline to pursue security because we do not like the available options. That can, and upon rare occasion has been tried, but we all should know that really bad things tend to happen to states that decline to defend themselves.

Any rational person, one might think, should be able to design a very much more reasonable and safer global security system than we have today. I suspect that this is true but alas, entirely beside the historical point. Our current security and insecurity context is the unplanned, certainly unintended, product of centuries of political history. As Professor Payne suggests in these pages, the best we can do is to make sensible use of our immense empirical experience. This will enable us to judge prudently what should, and what ought not be done as we strive, perhaps hopefully, to endure the darker possibilities of historical narrative.

Colin S. Gray
Professor Emeritus of Strategic Studies
University of Reading, UK

Preface

The nuclear policy debate in the United States includes a diverse set of policy questions, including: Should the United States seek as the priority to maintain nuclear weapons or to pursue nuclear disarmament? If the United States is to retain nuclear weapons, what is their purpose and how many of what type are needed to serve said purpose? How can the United States best approach a strategy of deterrence? Is deterrence an adequate U.S. strategy to prevent nuclear attack? Or, should the United States also pursue capabilities to physically defend against nuclear attack? These questions have been at the heart of a debate in the United States that has been ongoing for seven decades. While the United States now confronts many other defense policy issues, these strategic questions have resurfaced, seemingly abruptly, after several decades of quiescence born of the end of the Cold War and the associated prevalent Western expectation that nuclear matters were of ever-declining relevance to U.S. security.

The initial flowering of academic and official considerations of these questions took place in the 1950s and 1960s. The brilliant thinkers who devoted themselves to these subjects during those early years included Thomas Schelling, Bernard Brodie, Herman Kahn, and Albert Wohlstetter. They bequeathed to us a rich intellectual legacy, particularly regarding the subject of deterrence and its requirements. Together, they established the concepts and associated professional jargon that continue to dominate contemporary discussions. Their views differed greatly regarding how nuclear deterrence should be expected to function and best practices, but they clearly understood and engaged with each other — typically in an "old school" collegial manner that is less apparent in contemporary debate.

This book examines three different narratives that are the basis for three different sets of policy recommendations regarding deterrence and disarmament. These narratives include: 1) a nuclear disarmament narrative that often reflects basic axioms of Idealist thought; and, 2) two very different narratives regarding deterrence and its requirements that share some initial points of Realist thought—but sharply diverge thereafter. In these pages, these latter two competing narratives are labeled "easy" and "difficult" deterrence.

These three narratives have the same critical goal of preventing nuclear war but recommend very different policy paths to that end—ranging from the rejection of deterrence in favor of the priority pursuit of global nuclear disarmament, to the maintenance of robust, modern nuclear capabilities and additional strategic capabilities for physical defense. Such contrary policy recommendations tend to follow from their very different starting points about the character of the international system and likely leadership decision making.

One theme of this study is an emphasis on the need to understand these three narratives to comprehend the competing policy arguments in the contemporary debate. Any observer who wants to understand how seemingly equally-credentialed experts can make diametrically-opposed recommendations must first understand the competing narratives behind those recommendations. For example, opposing arguments for placing policy priority on global nuclear disarmament or on maintaining nuclear deterrence capabilities tend to fall in line with an Idealist or Realist narrative. And, arguments for and against the current plan to rebuild the full U.S. strategic nuclear triad tend to follow the difficult or easy deterrence narrative, respectively. Because the assumptions and logic of competing arguments are imbedded in the underlying narratives, but very rarely exposed, it is critical to recognize and understand the narratives behind the competing arguments. Observers need a narrative roadmap to understand the actual content of competing assertions. They must look behind the curtain.

Another theme of this study is its focus on the speculative nature of these three narratives. They include speculative starting points that drive their respective policy recommendations. Because policy formulation is about preparing for the future as opposed to explaining the past, there are many inherent unknowns and uncertainties involved. To plan for the future, some uncertainties must be set aside and presumptions about the future posited in their place. There must be some initial, speculative "terms of reference." The correspondingly unavoidable consequence, as Colin Gray observed, "...[is] that there can be no objectively correct answer. [Because] None of the candidate answers are testable, save by the verdict of future events."[1] The best that may be offered are suggestions about which direction may be most prudent based on inferences from the information now available. While I believe more vs. less-informed speculation is possible, when it comes to predicting the future functioning of deterrence against a yet-unknown opponent, in a yet-unknown context, over yet-unknown stakes, we are all amateurs looking at shadows on the wall.

This lack of certainty does not fit well with political demands for policy planners to identify with great confidence the specific effects of moving in one direction or another, but it may be the best that honestly is possible. While this work takes this caveat to heart, and refrains from confident assertions, it does try to suggest where prudence lies—with full recognition that even such caveated suggestions have embedded speculative assumptions about the future. The conclusions I ultimately reach largely are

---

[1] Colin S. Gray, *Strategic Planning and Defence: Meeting the Challenge of Uncertainty* (London: Oxford University Press, 2014), p. 2.

consistent with where I started before this work: nuclear war must be prevented and deterrence remains a critical tool for this purpose. However, this author now has a greater appreciation for how the initial speculative assumptions embedded in the competing narratives shape conflicting policy positions regarding deterrence and disarmament. Perhaps most importantly, an understanding of these three narratives and how they shape their respective policy positions regarding how best to prevent nuclear war leads to the conclusion that no side of the nuclear policy debate has a unique monopoly on logic or reason.

Fairfax, Virginia   *Keith B. Payne*

Acknowledgements

I began working on this book intermittently in 2015 and, beginning in mid-2018, had the opportunity to focus on it more consistently. Writing it has been a pleasure—the culmination of many years devoted to the subject of deterrence as a tool to prevent war. I would like to express my great appreciation to the institutions and individuals who made this book possible. First, I would like to thank the Sarah Scaife Foundation for generously providing the resources necessary for the research and writing of this book; it would not otherwise have been possible. Thanks too to the National Institute for Public Policy for providing a continuing professional home where writing a book that focuses on academic-oriented theories not only still is accepted but is applauded. In particular, the late Colin Gray not only was the author of many outstanding works cited in these pages, he graciously reviewed and provided helpful comments on early drafts of the text and his thoughtful *Foreword*—continuing the unparalleled mentorship and friendly guidance he gave me over the course of decades. Colin was one of the greatest scholars of strategy of our time and will be sorely missed. At National Institute, many thanks to Amy Joseph; she has been beyond patient and gracious in preparing the manuscript repeatedly as it evolved over years, with my endless footnotes, revisions, inserts and last-minute changes. I greatly appreciate Dr. Victor Matthews, of Missouri State University, for his consistent encouragement over the years. I also am very grateful for the many individuals whose comments on all or portions of the text prevented me from making mistakes and also pointed me toward needed changes, additions and deletions. My sincere thanks in this regard are to Stephen Cimbala, Matthew Costlow, Michaela Dodge, Eric Edelman, Michael Guillot, Kurt Guthe, Robert Joseph, Thomas Mahnken, Richard Mies, and David Trachtenberg, and also to several anonymous reviewers. Last, but most, I would like to thank my dear wife for so nicely putting up with my reading and writing at all hours, and for editing the entire manuscript twice. I would tell her that this is my final such effort, but she knows better.

"And I dreamed I saw the bombers, Riding shotgun in the sky, And they were turning into butterflies, Above our nation....We are golden, Caught in the devil's bargain, And we've got to get ourselves back to the garden."

Lyrics from *Woodstock*
by Joni Mitchell, 1969

"Out of the crooked timber of humanity, no straight thing was ever made."

Immanuel Kant, 1784

"In a world with no overarching global authority, rules are only as strong as the willingness of states to follow or enforce them."

U.S. Joint Chiefs of Staff, 2016

"To the realist, peace represents a stable balance of power; to the idealist, a goal so pre-eminent that it conceals the difficulty of finding the means to achieve it."

Henry Kissinger, 1973

Chapter 1
Idealism and Realism:
Competing Worldviews and Priorities

Introduction

In the marketplace of ideas two very different political philosophies have had overwhelming influence on Western thought about the nature and practice of international politics. These competing philosophies are commonly known as Realism and Idealism.

For the Realist, interstate conflicts of interest and the potential for aggression are constants inherent in an anarchic, "self-help" international system. The renowned, late Realist scholar, Kenneth Waltz explains why this is so: "With many sovereign states, with no law enforceable among them, with each state judging its grievances and ambitions according to the dictates of its own reason or desire — conflict, sometimes leading to war, is bound to occur."[1] Interstate cooperation cannot be assumed and no authority exists with the power and will to reliably prevent aggression. Consequently, while points of cooperation may exist, individual states ultimately are responsible for their own survival because no other reliable mechanism exists to protect them, and the pursuit of national power for self-preservation is the reasonable and prudent national priority.

In contrast, Idealists see the inherent dangers of an anarchic international system. They focus on the priority goal of transforming the system to achieve a cooperative order that facilitates and enforces the peaceful resolution of interstate conflicts. Idealists deem this transformation goal

---

[1] Kenneth Waltz, *Man, the State and War* (New York: Columbia University Press, 1954), p. 159.

to be feasible if national leaders will follow reason and enlightened self-interest. This is a goal that all reasonable parties should share because it would ease or eliminate the harsh security concerns otherwise imposed on states by the anarchic structure of the existing international system and the corresponding need for states to prioritize power and position over more noble and cooperative callings.

Idealists have pointed to different modes and paths for this transformation, but typically suggest that the dynamic for this transformation will be a common, reasoned response to the obvious need to establish a more peaceful and secure order. As a highly regarded mid-20th century historian, E. H. Carr, described this dynamic: "Reason could demonstrate the absurdity of the international anarchy; and with increasing knowledge, enough people would be rationally convinced of its absurdity to put an end to it."[2] Carr noted that the Idealist drive to do so flourished in Western countries following the horrific slaughter of World War I.   In particular, after that war, President Woodrow Wilson advanced the goal, logic and arguments of Idealism in his great efforts to establish the League of Nations — an international organization that he intended to provide collective security for all states via the power of world public opinion, economic sanctions, and military force if necessary.[3] President Wilson spoke of his efforts in personal, even Messianic terms: "Why has Jesus Christ so far not succeeded in inducing the world to follow his teachings in these matters? It is because he taught the ideal without devising any practical means for attaining it. That is why I am proposing a practical scheme to carry out His aims."[4]

---

[2] Edward Hallett Carr, *The Twenty Years' Crisis, 1919-1939* (New York: Harper and Row, 1964), p. 26.

[3] Ibid., pp. 8-18, 27-36.

[4] Quoted in John G. Stoessinger, *Why Nations Go To War*, Tenth Edition (Belmont, CA: Thomas Wadsworth, 2008), p. 325.

In short, whereas Realists see states as compelled to pursue power and position given the unavoidable potential for conflict and aggression in an anarchic international system, Idealists see the potential for its profound transformation to a more cooperative and peaceful order — allowing states to reduce or even eliminate the pursuit of national power and position as the priority. Realism and Idealism provide contrary starting points about the nature of international politics that lead to equally contrary analyses and conclusions about national leadership best practices. Indeed, while both Realists and Idealists include eminent scholars and statesmen, they often see precisely the same set of international circumstances and draw wholly contradictory conclusions about the meaning of those circumstances and the most reasonable courses of action in those circumstances.

That these two competing schools of thought often yield wholly different analyses, conclusions and policy directions is nowhere more apparent than in debates about nuclear weapons and nuclear deterrence. Public debate on nuclear policies often is wrapped in jargon and advocacy; the significance of Realism and Idealism to the subject is rarely part of the discussion.[5] This general lack of recognition or

---

[5] For exceptions to this rule see Campbell Craig, *Glimmer of a New Leviathan* (New York: Columbia University Press, 2003); Colin Gray, "Through a Missile Tube Darkly: 'New' Thinking about Nuclear Strategy," *Political Studies*, No. XLI (1993), pp. 661-671; John Deutch, "The Future of the U.S. Nuclear Deterrent," *The National Interest* (April 4, 2017), available at http://national interest.org/feature/the-future-the-us-nuclear deterrent-2020?page=show; Rebeccah Heinrichs, "U.S. Foreign Policy Is Overdue For Some Realism," *RealClearDefense*, August 16, 2015, available at http://.realclear defense.com/articles/2015/08/16/us_foreign_policy_is_overdue_for_some_realism_108368.html; Keith Payne, "US Nuclear Weapons and Deterrence: Realist Versus Utopian Thinking," *Air and Space Power Journal* (July-August 2015), pp. 63-71; and Stephen Cimbala, "Nuclear Proliferation in the Twenty-First Century: Realism, Rationality, or

acknowledgement of the Realist or Idealist connection to competing nuclear narratives obscures an understanding of the assumptions, logic, strengths and weaknesses of those narratives. Consideration of competing narratives about nuclear weapons and deterrence that ignores their Realist or Idealist roots will miss much of the story, and likely lead to conclusions that are significantly uninformed. The goal here is not to review all the academic variations and nuances of Idealism and Realism. Rather it is to identify the connections of competing nuclear narratives to general Realist and Idealist thought, and by doing so to help provide a more complete understanding of those narratives and a more complete framework for considering them.

The Transformation of the International Order and Nuclear Disarmament

A well-developed nuclear disarmament narrative contends that disarmament is a matter of existential importance because individual state deployment of nuclear arsenals poses an extreme and immediate risk to humanity: "All nuclear weapons are a humanitarian threat…designed to lay waste to cities and indiscriminately mass murder civilians."[6] Consequently, this narrative concludes with the corresponding policy prescription that the pursuit of complete nuclear disarmament should be the U.S. policy

---

Uncertainty?" *Strategic Studies Quarterly*, Vol. 11, No. 1 (Spring 2019), pp. 129-146.

[6] Beatrice Fihn, "Confronting Russia's Nuclear Aggression," *U.S. News and World Report*, March 5, 2019, at https://www.usnews.com/news/best-countries/articles/2019-03-05/commentary-nations-should-use-international-law-to-stop-russian-nuclear-aggression.

priority and, indeed, the priority goal of all states in the international system.[7]

Idealism often is the explicit or implicit philosophical position underlying this nuclear disarmament narrative. It essentially adopts Idealism and contends that the existing international system of independent and often conflicting states *can be transformed* via concerted, cooperative international efforts to such a degree that individual states ultimately will no longer feel compelled to, or need to, maintain independent nuclear arsenals. The felt need to maintain nuclear weapons can be relieved by alternative global security mechanisms and anti-nuclear norms that advance and codify the common desire to eliminate nuclear weapons and thus the risks they pose to all humanity. This can be done cooperatively because it is in each state's enlightened self-interest to do so given the global threat posed by the existence of nuclear weapons.

This disarmament narrative, in common with Idealist thought in general, places considerable emphasis on the transformative power of reason, enlightened self-interest, and the instruments of collective security or "cooperative security," international institutions, laws and norms. These are the mechanisms that have the potential to so transform the international system.[8] The rudiments of these

---

[7] See for example, Richard Falk and David Krieger, *The Path to Zero* (Boulder, CO: Paradigm Publishers, 2012).

[8] For a useful discussion of a U.N.-enforced global "cooperative security" regime reached via international consensus and consent that military preparation will be limited to territorial defense see Ashton Carter, John Steinbruner, and William Perry, *A New Concept of Cooperative Security* (Washington, D.C.: Brookings Institution, January 1992), pp. 7-20. For a still useful discussion of how nuclear deterrence could be "to some degree supplanted" by a fundamentally more cooperative international system see, David Welch, "Internationalism: Contacts, Trade, and Institutions," in *Fateful Visions: Avoiding Nuclear Catastrophe*, Joseph Nye, Graham Allison, and Albert Carnesale, eds. (Cambridge, MA: Ballinger Publishing Company, 1988), pp. 171-196.

mechanisms and corresponding transition purportedly already are visible in the rise of international institutions, the decline in interstate wars and combat deaths over decades, the workings of the United Nations, multilateral arms control agreements, and the spread of democratic governments.[9]

The expressed need for such a transformation and belief in its practical feasibility is reflected in President Obama's well-crafted and Idealist-oriented 2016 speech to the United Nations. He offers the promise that leaders of good will can transform the international system.

> We are all stakeholders in this international system, and it calls upon us to invest in the success of [international] institutions to which we belong...I recognize history tells a different story than the one that I've talked about here today. There is a darker and more cynical view of history that we can adopt....We have to remember that the choices of individual human beings led to repeated world war.

---

[9] In 2015, then-Under Secretary of State Rose Gottemoeller said that the world had avoided nuclear war "because we created an intricate and essential system of treaties, laws and agreements that control the world's most destructive weapons... Our goal is a safe and secure world without nuclear weapons and we are capable of getting there." See, Rose Gottemoeller, *Arms Control Priorities for Russia and the United States in 2015 and Beyond*, February 18, 2015, available at http://www.state.govt/us/2015/237581.htm. Then-U.S. Secretary of State John Kerry assured an audience of international notables that "the vast majority of the world" had come to the conclusion that "nuclear weapons should one day be eliminated," and that "moral leadership is more powerful than any weapon." He added that embracing "a notion of change in how we resolve conflicts, in how we think, in how we conduct our daily global affairs" can indeed create "a future in which nuclear weapons exist only within the pages of history books." Secretary of State John Kerry, *Remarks at the 2015 Nuclear Nonproliferation Treaty Review Conference*, New York City, April 27, 2015, at http://www.state.gov/secretary/remarks/2015/04/241175.htm.

But we also have to remember that the choices of individual human beings created a United Nations, so that a war like that would never happen again. Each of us as leaders, each nation can choose to reject those who appeal to our worst impulses and embrace those who appeal to our best. For we have shown that we can choose a better history.[10]

A well-noted 1960 text by Grenville Clark and Louis Sohn, *World Peace Through World Law*, laid out in great detail the legal framework and requirements for an international organization with the authority and police power needed to enforce the general disarmament of all states and peaceful interstate relations — effectively transforming the international system by eliminating the national security concerns that are so central to Realist thought.[11] *World Peace Through World Law* presents the underlying principles and main features of such a transformed global collective security organization, with the hopeful prediction that by 1975 it would be "well on its way."[12]

The disarmament narrative acknowledges the reality that international threats can drive national leaders' felt need for nuclear weapons to help address their respective security concerns. But this reality does not justify the continued pursuit or maintenance of national nuclear capabilities: "These are valid points, but they do not diminish the necessity of disarmament. Acknowledgement

---

[10] Barack Obama, "Address by President Obama to the 71st Session of the United Nations General Assembly," WhiteHouse.gov, September 20, 2016, available at https://obamawhitehouse.archives.gov/the-press-office/2016/09/20/address-president-obama-71st-session-united-nations-general-assembly.

[11] Grenville Clark and Louis Sohn, *World Peace Through World Law* (Cambridge, MA: Harvard University Press, 1960).

[12] Ibid, pp. xliii-xliv.

of fundamental security realities makes nuclear disarmament more, not less, urgent."[13]

The disarmament narrative's contention is that the continued existence of nuclear weapons now poses a greater security risk to states than would their voluntary nuclear disarmament. Indeed, the risk posed by the existence of nuclear arsenals is unprecedented and should establish the dynamic for the equally unprecedented level of interstate cooperation necessary for nuclear disarmament: the need to address the nuclear risk should overshadow other national security fears and drive the level of interstate cooperation needed for disarmament.

The relationship between the prospects for disarmament and a cooperative international political order has long been recognized. A highly regarded, 1941 academic study of international arms control efforts following World War I reached this conclusion: [14]

> Any diminution in the relative armament strength of a state means a proportionately diminished ability to carry its national policies through to what it regards as a successful conclusion. Conference delegates are determined to maintain and are disposed to increase, their nation's armament power *relative* to that of other states; hence they scrutinize every scheme of reduction with minute care, and uncharitably search for the special motive prompting its proposal. Pervaded by this atmosphere of mutual distrust, disarmament

---

[13] David Cortright and Raimo Väyrynen, *Towards Nuclear Zero* (New York: Routledge, 2010), p. 20.

[14] See Marion William Boggs, *Attempts to Define and Limit "Aggressive" Armament in Diplomacy and Strategy*, The University of Missouri Studies, Vol. 16, No. 1 (Columbia: University of Missouri, 1941).

gatherings are led to discuss the means of waging war under the name of peace.

...Evidently the [necessary] conditions of peace include not only the stable balance of power...but also a system of international law intolerant of violence, a desire for peace in the human population superior to all conflicting desires, and an organization of the world community adequate to restrain hostilities.

....The present epoch may be a period of transition in world history — transition from the exclusive pursuit of national interest, with war as an accepted instrument of national policy, to the cooperative establishment of the conditions of peace. But the latter goal is not yet in sight; it remains a period of transition.[15]

In 1983, the U.S. Conference of Catholic Bishops issued a Pastoral Letter regarding nuclear weapons and deterrence. It concluded with a conditional endorsement of nuclear deterrence as a step en route to disarmament in a transformed international system: "There is a substitute for war. There is negotiation under the supervision of a global body realistically fashioned to do its job. It must be given the equipment to keep constant surveillance on the entire earth. Present technology makes this possible. It must be empowered by all the nations to enforce its commands on every nation."[16]

The contemporary disarmament narrative contends that the catalyst for the needed transformation is recognition of the potential for a global nuclear catastrophe. When leaders understand the severity of the common threat posed by the

---

[15] Ibid., pp. 102-104. (Emphasis in original).

[16] See the U.S. Catholic Bishops' Pastoral Letter in, "The Challenge of Peace: God's Promise and Our Response," *Origins* (May 19, 1983), p. 30.

existence of nuclear weapons, they should be willing to engage in nuclear disarmament in their own enlightened self-interest. That is, the common threat posed by the existence of nuclear weapons can overcome national leaders' felt need to sustain them for national security purposes, and inspire the unprecedented interstate cooperation needed to transform the system and realize nuclear disarmament:

> To reach nuclear zero it is necessary to achieve what Professor Jonathan Schell describes as political zero, a state of political relations among nations in which there is no desire or need to possess nuclear weapons, where tensions and animosities that lead nations to fear their neighbors have declined towards zero. Political zero does not mean that nations live in a world without conflicts; it only means the risks of conflict can be limited in a system where certain mechanisms exist to prevent them from escalating to dangerous levels.[17]

Thus the emphasis is on the transformation of the international system as necessary to enable global nuclear disarmament, and the fear of a global nuclear catastrophe is the catalyst that should drive that transformation. Because of the unprecedented severity of the common nuclear threat to all countries, the transformation of the international system needed for nuclear disarmament should be feasible with informed leaders *behaving reasonably and with courage*. Proponents of disarmament emphasize that the national security fears driving the desire for nuclear capabilities may be overcome to enable nuclear disarmament via "strategic

---

[17] Cortright and Väyrynen, op. cit., p. 21.

foresight and political courage:"[18] "It is ideas…rather than technical problems, that present the most difficult barriers to reaching [nuclear] zero. These are problems that can be overcome. No law of nature stands in the way."[19]

This disarmament narrative recognizes that the cooperative international transformation needed has not occurred in history and would need to proceed incrementally, but contends that given the common and unprecedented threat to all humanity posed by nuclear weapons, moving in this direction can proceed with broader recognition of that nuclear threat and the enlightened leadership needed to implement the transformation.[20] This transformation can reduce or eliminate the felt security requirement of individual states for nuclear weapons and deterrence, and enable the common good of eliminating the risks to all states and peoples posed by the existence of nuclear weapons.

The initial process of disarming, driven by the global fear of nuclear weapons, can be a dynamic for the further cooperative transformation of the international system.[21] As a noted journalist has suggested, "Maybe this is how a new sort of world, with foundations planted in human solidarity and connectedness, will come into being. Maybe

---

[18] James E. Goodby, *Approaching the Nuclear Tipping Point: Cooperative Security in an Era of Global Change* (New York: Rowman & Littlefield, 2017), p. 130.

[19] Ibid., p. 148.

[20] This point is elaborated well in, Falk and Krieger, *The Path to Zero*, p. 201; and Richard Falk and David Krieger, "Introduction," in Richard Falk and David Krieger, eds., *At the Nuclear Precipice: Catastrophe or Transformation?* (New York: Palgrave Macmillan, 2008).

[21] See James Acton, "Bombs Away? Being Realistic about Deep Nuclear Reductions," *The Washington Quarterly*, Vol. 35, No. 2 (Spring 2012), p. 50.

this is the true value of nuclear weapons: scare us into learning how to get along."[22]

Correspondingly, frequently expressed goals of the nuclear disarmament narrative include: 1) the global promotion of recognition of the inherent risks to all posed by the existence of nuclear weapons, and the consequent need for transforming international relations to enable their elimination; and, 2) organizing political pressure on national leaders to move in this direction. There are many examples of this argument in action, including the relatively recent U.S. official and popular advocacy of "nuclear zero,"[23] and the contemporary UN-based Treaty on the Prohibition of Nuclear Weapons:[24] "International norms influence all states...There must be a global embrace of the UN's Treaty on the Prohibition of Nuclear Weapons, which sets these norms against nuclear weapons."[25] As Treaty proponent Beatrice Fihn, Executive Director of the International Campaign to Abolish Nuclear Weapons, stated in her 2017 Nobel Peace Prize acceptance speech:

> We represent the *only* rational choice... Ours is the only reality that is possible. The alternative is

---

[22] Robert Koehler, "Nuclear Realism," *The Blog*, May 15, 2015, at https://www.huffingtonpost.com/entry/nuclear-realism_b_7470252.

[23] See for example, Ivo Daalder and Jan Lodal, "The Logic of Zero," *Foreign Affairs* (November-December 2008), pp. 80-95. "As a critical element of our effort to move toward a world free of nuclear weapons, the United States will lead expanded international efforts to rebuild and strengthen the global nuclear non-proliferation regime—and for the first time, the 2010 NPR places this priority atop the U.S. nuclear policy agenda." See, U.S. Department of Defense, *Nuclear Posture Review Report*, April 2010, p. vi.

[24] See for example, Zia Mian, "After the Nuclear Weapons Ban Treaty: A New Disarmament Politics," *Bulletin of the Atomic Scientists*, July 7, 2017, at http://thebulletin.org/after-the-nuclear-weapons-ban-treaty-new-disarmament-politics10932.

[25] Fihn, op. cit.

unthinkable. The story of nuclear weapons will
have an ending, and it is up to us what that ending
will be. Will it be the end of nuclear weapons, or
will it be the end of us?... The Treaty on the
Prohibition of Nuclear Weapons provides the
pathway forward at a moment of great global crisis.
It is a light in a dark time. And more than that, it
provides a choice. A choice between the two
endings: the end of nuclear weapons or the end of
us. It is not naïve to believe in the first choice. It is
not irrational to think nuclear states can disarm. It is
not idealistic to believe in life over fear and
destruction; *it is a necessity.*[26]

The modern "nuclear zero" movement was endorsed
very publicly by President Obama, with Realist caveats, in
his famous 2009 Prague Speech.[27] Unsurprisingly, this
nuclear disarmament initiative subsequently received an
unparalleled level of favorable public and media attention.
As Yale Professor Paul Bracken observed: "All were on
board to oppose nuclear arms... Academics, think tanks
and intellectuals quickly jumped on the bandwagon. For a
time, it really looked like there was going to be an
antinuclear turn in U.S. strategy."[28]

---

[26] Beatrice Fihn, "International Campaign to Abolish Nuclear Weapons
(ICAN) – Nobel Lecture (English)," *NobelPrize.org*, December 10, 2017,
available at
https://www.nobelprize.org/prizes/peace/2017/ican/26041-
international-campaign-to-abolish-nuclear-weapons-ican-nobel-lecture-
2017/. Emphasis in original.

[27] See The White House, Office of the Press Secretary, *Remarks by
President Barack Obama, Hradcany Square, Prague, Czech Republic*, April 5,
2009.

[28] Paul Bracken, "Whatever Happened to Nuclear Abolition?," *The Hill*,
March 19, 2019, available at https://thehill.com/opinion/national-
security/434723-whatever-happened-to-nuclear-abolition.

Well before 2009, however, scholars of international relations suggested the viability of an Idealist-oriented path for transforming the international system to achieve the goal of nuclear disarmament. For example:

> If the roots of the nuclear problem lie in a pathological national-state system, then we need to do no more (and should do no less) than change that system. Some of the necessary changes have been recognized for a century or more. Foremost among them is strengthening international authority so that it can provide an effective system of security for all nations….if citizens' movements can force nations to follow through on creating an effective international security organization, they can pull the deadly fangs of the nation-state system.[29]

Also, in 2009, then-Director of the International Atomic Energy Agency, Mohamed El Baradei, pointed to the need for an effective global collective security system to enable nuclear disarmament: "We need a return to a system rooted in effective multilateralism. The [United Nations] Security Council must be drastically reformed so the world can rely on it as the primary body for maintaining international peace and security, as foreseen in the UN Charter."[30]

El Baradei's point here nicely reflects the fundamentals of Idealist thought as applied to the question of nuclear disarmament: when *a global organization* (in this case, the UN) is able to maintain "international peace and security" reliably, states in the system will no longer confront

---

[29] Lawrence Wittner, *The Struggle Against the Bomb, Volume Three: Toward Nuclear Abolition* (Stanford, CA: Stanford University Press, 2003), pp. 490-491.

[30] Mohamed El Baradei, "Five Steps Towards Abolishing Nuclear Weapons," *Sueddeutsche Zeitung*, April 2, 2009, at http://www.sueddeutsche.de/politik/629/457290/text/.

dominating security concerns and will, therefore, be free to disarm without fear.

The nuclear disarmament narrative often refers to national policies of nuclear deterrence as an impediment to progress towards nuclear disarmament and an unworthy and short-sighted rationale for sustaining nuclear weapons. A policy of nuclear deterrence is deemed an impediment to disarmament because it suggests a positive, important value for nuclear weapons in contrast to the establishment of a global norm against them. Consequently, the argument for nuclear disarmament often includes a critique of nuclear deterrence (the primary justification for nuclear weapons) as being an unnecessary, unreliable and accident-prone security strategy. The point is that were national leaders to set aside nuclear deterrence policies, there ostensibly would be little or no loss of national security because nuclear deterrence is unnecessary and/or unreliable. In return, countries would benefit from the elimination of the risk of nuclear accidents and an easing of the way to global nuclear disarmament. This trade-off is the great net benefit of pursuing disarmament as the priority, and not deterrence: little or nothing of value would be lost, in exchange for a gain of inestimable value.

In short, advocates of nuclear disarmament often become critics of nuclear deterrence and present the prioritization of nuclear deterrence or nuclear disarmament policies as mutually exclusive choices, with the obvious conclusion that disarmament is the only sensible choice. For example:

> Nuclear deterrence comes with tremendous risks and costs. The arguments in favor of deterrence, if sometimes true, are not likely to be true in every case. What happens when it fails? The growing risk of a catastrophic nuclear war outweighs the

uncertain benefits of deterrence for the United States.[31]

Nuclear deterrence is the heart of the nuclear believers' case; it's their indispensable idea, and without it, they have nothing. Nuclear deterrence is indefensible because 1) we don't understand it, 2) it has failed in the past, and 3) it will inevitably fail in the future.[32]

They made us false promises. That by making the consequences of using these weapons so unthinkable it would make any conflict unpalatable. That it would keep us free from war. But far from preventing war, these weapons brought us to the brink multiple times throughout the Cold War. And in this century, these weapons continue to escalate us towards war and conflict.[33]

Nuclear deterrence does not provide physical protection against nuclear weapons — it provides only a false sense of security and the possibility of retaliation and vengeance. Reliance on nuclear deterrence opens the door to omnicide.[34]

Indeed, some nuclear disarmament proponents suggest that those who have great confidence in deterrence working

---

[31] Nina Tannenwald, "The Vanishing Nuclear Taboo?," *Foreign Affairs*, Vol. 97, No. 6 (November-December 2018), pp. 22, 23-24.

[32] Ward Wilson, "Making the Realist Case Against Nuclear Weapons," November 13, 2015, at http://www.globalzero.org/blog/making-realistic-case-against-nuclear-weapons.

[33] Fihn, "International Campaign to Abolish Nuclear Weapons (ICAN) — Nobel Lecture," op. cit.

[34] David Krieger, "10 Lessons You Should Learn About Nuclear Weapons," *The Hill*, February 15, 2019, available at https://thehill.com/opinion/national-security/430296-10-lessons-you-should-learn-about-nuclear-weapons.

reliably to prevent war are "nuclear romantics," *not Realists*, because such confidence is based on unrealistic expectations of leaders consistently behaving prudently and sensibly.[35] Nuclear deterrence policies and weapons are a problem. The transformation of the international system and disarmament are the answer.

Realist Thought and Cooperative Global Transformation

In 1962, the renowned Realist academic, Hans Morgenthau, observed that, "The history of modern political thought is the story of a contest between two schools that differ fundamentally in their conceptions of the nature of man, society, and politics."[36] Arnold Wolfers, another highly regarded 20th century political theorist, noted similarly: "In international relations, two opposing schools of thought have fought each other throughout the modern age. Ever since Machiavelli published *The Prince*, his 'realistic' views have shocked 'idealist' thinkers...Today, more than ever American statesmen and the American public find themselves torn between the conflicting pulls of idealist and realist thought."[37]

Decades later, at the beginning of the new millennium, the same point held true. The study of international relations, "...can be reduced to two broad, internally rich and competing conceptions of the subject: idealism and

---

[35] For example, Ward Wilson, "How Nuclear Realists Falsely Frame the Nuclear Weapons Debate," May 7, 2015, available at https://thebulletin.org/2015/05/how-the-nuclear-realists-falsely-frame-the-nuclear-weapons-debate/.

[36] Hans Morgenthau, *Politics Among Nations: The Struggle for Power and Peace* (New York: Alfred Knopf, 1962), p. 3.

[37] Arnold Wolfers, "The Pole of Power and the Pole of Indifference," in, James Rosenau, ed., *International Politics and Foreign Policy* (London: The Free Press, 1969), p. 175.

realism."[38]   And,   "...idealism   and   realism   are
fundamentally at odds with one another, and cannot be
reconciled in theory or practice...the clash between idealists
and realists is an ontological foundation predicated on
conflicting   assessments   of   human   nature   and   the
possibilities for, and appropriate conceptions of progress in
international relations."[39]

Realist thought, while quite varied, is based on the
proposition that the international system is an anarchic,
"self-help" system because cooperation cannot be assumed
and there is no overarching authority with sufficient power
to regulate interstate behavior reliably and predictably.[40]
Most importantly, no global organization exists that is
capable of reliably preventing interstate aggression.
Because conflicts of interest among states are inevitable, the
absence of an overarching organization with authority and
power leaves open the constant opportunity for aggression
and war by any state so inclined.   As Robert Jervis has
noted, "For realists, world politics is a continuing if not an

---

[38] Robert Crawford, *Idealism and Realism in International Relations:
Beyond the Discipline* (London: Routledge, 2000), p. 15.

[39] Ibid., p. 4.

[40] See, for example, Hans Morgenthau, op. cit., pp. 3-15; Kenneth Waltz,
Man, the State and War, op. cit., especially chapters VII and VIII; Edward
Hallett Carr, *The Twenty Years' Crisis, 1919-1939*, op. cit., especially pp.
1-94; Raymond Aron, *Peace and War: A Theory of International Relations*
(Paris, Calmann-Levy: 1962); and, Hedley Bull, *The Anarchical Society*
(New York: Columbia University Press, 1977), especially Part I. There
are multiple variations of Realism. But the anarchic character of
interstate relations and its effects are a common theme. For more recent
helpful discussions of Realism and its variants see, Robert Jervis,
"Realism, Neoliberalism, and Cooperation," *International Security*, Vol.
24, No. 1 (Summer 1999), pp. 42-63; John J. Mearsheimer, *The Tragedy of
Great Power Politics* (New York: W. W. Norton & Company, 2001); and,
John J. Mearsheimer, "E.H. Carr vs Idealism: The Battle Rages On,"
Security Studies, Vol. 19, No. 2 (2005), pp. 139-152.

unrelenting struggle for survival, advantage, and often dominance."[41]

This is not to suggest that Realism contends that there are no international institutions, laws, norms or possible points of trust and cooperation. That these exist is self-evident. However, in an anarchic international system, as states encounter conflicts of interest, each state ultimately has the prerogative to decide its own course of action for good or ill and there is no international authority with sufficient unity of will and power to enforce reliably international laws and norms.

Individual states ultimately also are "on their own" with regard to their protection from external threats. Alliances and diplomacy certainly can ease national security concerns, but historical evidence demonstrates convincingly that neither is fully reliable to provide protection from external threats. Alliances periodically fail to protect and diplomacy is conducted under the shadow of and influenced by power relations. Victor Davis Hanson of Stanford University's Hoover Institution reflects this Realist thought: "In sophisticated times, we sometimes forget that time-honored concepts like the balance of power and military deterrence — not good intentions and international peace organizations — alone keep the peace."[42]

Consequently, states seek power to provide for their own security, but in doing so may drive the suspicions and fears of others concerned about their own relative power positions.[43] States seeking no more than their own security

---

[41] Jervis, op. cit., pp. 44-45.

[42] Victor Davis Hanson, "Lies, Betrayal and Incredible Surprises Marked Start of World War II 80 Years Ago," *Tribune Media Services*, August 15, 2019, available at https://www.foxnews.com/opinion/victor-davis-hanson-world-war-ii.

[43] For a useful discussion of this "security dilemma" see, Robert Jervis, "Cooperation Under the Security Dilemma," *World Politics*, Vol. 30, No. 3 (January 1978), pp. 186-214.

can drive other states' perceptions of insecurity as each must be watchful of the other in a lawless system. Because the international system is anarchic and dangerous in this sense, each state must be concerned about its power position relative to any other state that is, or might become, a security threat. As Kenneth Waltz has observed: "States coexist in a condition of anarchy. Self-help is the principle of action in an anarchic order, and the most important way in which states must help themselves is by providing for their own security."[44]

According to this Realist axiom, in response to the condition of international anarchy each state has an overarching interest in its power position (defined as the capability to control others). Where there is no central authority with the will and power needed to enforce rules and cooperation, the accumulation of power is necessary for those states that perceive threats and give priority to their own survival. Hans Morgenthau refers to this as "interest defined as power."[45] In the international sphere, state leaders generally will, to the extent feasible, seek power in response to the threat levels they perceive or anticipate. Leaders generally also will subordinate, if necessary, other possible goals, such as adherence to international norms or legal standards, to the accumulation of and use of power necessary to provide for national survival. As University of Chicago professor John Mearsheimer concludes, "States operating in a self-help world almost always act according to their own self-interest and do not subordinate their interests to the interests of other states, or to the interests of the so-called international community."[46]

---

[44] Kenneth Waltz, "The Spread of Nuclear Weapons: More May be Better," *Adelphi Papers*, Number 171 (London: International Institute for Strategic Studies, 1981), available at https://www.mtholyoke.edu/acad/intrel/waltz1.htm.

[45] Morgenthau, op. cit., p. 5.

[46] Mearsheimer, *The Tragedy of Great Power Politics*, op. cit., p. 33.

Realists generally contend that this is not an immoral, ignorant or malicious approach to international relations. Rather, it is a reasonable and prudent response to the reality of an anarchic international system and the security concerns it imposes on virtually all states. Morgenthau explains in this regard that the standards by which national political leaders must judge their international behavior are different from those of the lawyer, moralist or religious leader.[47] Political leaders must place national survival and the necessary tools of power for that survival as their priority goals, subordinating if necessary other possible national goals to this end, including adherence to international norms or legal codes. As the late Oxford History professor, Sir Michael Howard observed:

> Those responsible for the conduct of state affairs see their first duty as being to ensure that their state survives; that it retains its power to protect its members and provide for them the conditions of a good life. For the individual, personal survival is not necessarily the highest duty. He may well feel called upon to sacrifice himself to his ideals, his family, or his friends. The state, or those responsible for it, cannot.[48]

The "real-world" manifestation of this point is evidenced repeatedly across time and cultures. For example, in 1941, Japanese War Minister Hideki Tojo presented the planned attack on Pearl Harbor to Prince Fumimaro Konoye in personal, high-risk terms: "Sometimes it is necessary for a man to risk his life in one leap." In response, Konoye "reminded the general that a

---

[47] Morgenthau, op. cit., p. 10.

[48] Michael Howard, *Studies in War and Peace* (New York: Viking Press, 1964), p. 238.

metaphor must not be carried too far, that 'crossing the Rubicon' and 'risking the fate of the nation' were exciting words, but that starting a war without seeing the prospect of success is very different from the case of an individual. At last, when one thinks of the 2600-year-old faultless national policy, one cannot act so irresponsibly. Even when criticized as slow or old-fashioned, people like myself cannot act in such a way."[49]

In short, national leaders do not have the prerogative to subordinate the goal of protecting those under their authority against foreign threats to other goals if doing so would threaten national survival. To do so would be to abdicate their most basic leadership responsibilities of protecting innocent citizens in a dangerous international system. In contrast, the lawyer may see adherence to legal codes as the highest-priority goal, the moralist adherence to moral standards, and the religious leader adherence to religious standards.

Realism provides this logical explanation for why states often pursue national power and subordinate other goals to that end. Doing so can be a prudent and reasonable response to the anarchic character and security dilemma of the international system. Realists contend that the "accumulated experience of the ages" is evidence supporting this explanation and conclusion.[50] They point out that in severe security crises across time and place, international cooperative norms and legal structures have been subordinated to the national security imperative of the hour. Hence, in 1914 Imperial Germany justified its violation of Belgium's codified neutrality as necessary in defense of its national security. In 1940, democratic Great Britain violated Norway's neutrality to check the expansion

---

[49] Alfred Vagts, *Defense and Diplomacy: The Soldier and the Conduct of Foreign Relations* (New York: King's Crown Press, 1956), p. 370.

[50] Waltz, quoting John Jay's *Federalist* (Number 5), in Waltz, *Man, the State and War*, op. cit., p. 237.

of German power, and killed almost 1,300 French naval personnel in its attack on the French naval base at Mers-el-Kébir. Britain took the latter action against its erstwhile ally for fear that the French fleet would otherwise fall into German hands and tip the naval balance in favor of Germany. The respective German and British justifications for these military actions were similar — that is, the highest calling of national security demanded them. As the German Chancellor Theobald von Bethmann-Hollweg openly said to the Reichstag on 4 August 1914: "Gentlemen, we are in a state of necessity, and necessity knows no law. Our troops have already entered Belgium territory... He who is menaced as we are and is fighting for his highest possession can only consider how he is to hack his way through."[51]

Even in less severe circumstances, countries often subordinate their commitments to international norms and laws if necessary to advance their national security goals. This is illustrated in the contemporary period by Russia's apparent violations of various nuclear arms control treaties,[52] and China's explicit disregard of the 2016

---

[51] Theobald von Bethmann-Hollweg's speech is reprinted in, Roderick Ogley, *The Theory and Practice of Neutrality in the Twentieth Century* (New York: Routledge & K. Paul, 1970), p. 83. Winston Churchill's justification for British violation of Norwegian neutrality in 1940 was similar in essence: "We have a right, and indeed are duty bound, to abrogate for a space some of the conventions of the very laws we seek to consolidate and reaffirm... the letter of the law must not in supreme emergency obstruct those who are charged with its protection and enforcement." Winston S. Churchill, *The Gathering Storm* (Boston: Houghton Mifflin Co., 1948), p. 492.

[52] See, Daniel Coats, "Director of National Intelligence Daniel Coats on Russia's INF Treaty Violation," *DNI.gov*, November 30, 2018, available at https://www.dni.gov/index.php/newsroom/speeches-interviews/item/1923-director-of-national-intelligence-daniel-coats-on-russias-inf-treaty-violation; and Defense Intelligence Agency, "DIA Statement on Lt. Gen. Ashley's Remarks at Hudson Institute," *DIA.mil*, June 13, 2019, available at https://www.dia.mil/News/Speeches-and-Testimonies/Article-View/Article/1875351/dia-statement-on-lt-gen-ashleys-remarks-at-hudson-institute/; and Paul Sonne, "U.S. Military

rejection of its sweeping sovereignty claims in the South China Sea by the Permanent Court of Arbitration in the Hague.[53]

The Realist challenge confronting the Idealist nuclear disarmament narrative is the contention that the cooperative transformation of the anarchic international system to one that is reliably secure and enables nuclear disarmament is implausible, if not impossible, in any anticipated time frame. And, in the absence of such a transformation, some states will continue to ease their security concerns via the maintenance of nuclear capabilities for deterrence and/or coercive purposes. Initiatives that place *policy priority* on the U.S. pursuit of nuclear disarmament over sustaining nuclear deterrence capabilities may be misguided and possibly dangerous because the underlying timely international transformation necessary for general nuclear disarmament *simply is not plausible*.

The central importance to the nuclear debate of these basic philosophical positions about what is and is not plausible is reflected in the following statement from the 2009 final report of the Bipartisan Strategic Nuclear Posture Commission (the Perry-Schlesinger Commission): "The conditions that might make possible the global elimination of nuclear weapons are not present today and their creation

---

Intelligence Steps Up Accusations Against Russia Over Nuclear Testing," *The Washington Post*, June 13, 2009, at https://www.washingtonpost.com/world/national-security/us-military-intelligence-steps-up-accusation-against-russia-over-nuclear-testing/2019/06/13/2dadf2e2-8e26-11e9-b162-8f6f41ec3c04_story.html.

[53] Jane Perlez, "Beijing's South China Sea Claims Rejected by Hague Tribunal," *The New York Times*, July 12, 2016, available at https://www.nytimes.com/2016/07/13/world/asia/south-china-sea-hague-ruling-philippines.html.

would require a fundamental transformation of the world political order."[54]

Such a statement is directly from the Realist canon: only when international relations are transformed so that member states no longer confront security threats and no longer believe themselves "on their own" will they reasonably eliminate the capabilities they consider essential to their security. Nuclear disarmament could ultimately be a consequence of such a transformation, *but disarmament cannot precede that transformation.*

Indeed, calling on states to disarm without the prior cooperative transformation of the anarchic interstate system is asking them to take imprudent risks with their own survival. States confronting existing or prospective security threats, particularly including nuclear threats, cannot reasonably be expected to accept such risks. Why? Mohammed El Baradei has provided a Realist-oriented answer, "We still live in a world where if you have nuclear weapons, you are buying power, you are buying insurance against attack."[55] Or, as University of Chicago professor John Mearsheimer says, "Nuclear weapons are considered the ultimate deterrent for good reason: Adversaries are unlikely to threaten the existence of a nuclear-armed state."[56]

For the Realist, nuclear weapons *are a symptom* of the enduring realities of the international system: conflicting interests, a continuing security dilemma and the enduring

---

[54] Congressional Commission on the Strategic Posture of the United States, *America's Strategic Posture* (Washington, D.C.: U.S. Institute of Peace, 2009), p. xvi.

[55] Quoted in, Julian Borger, "Mohamed El Baradei Warns of New Nuclear Age," *The Guardian*, May 14, 2009.

[56] John J. Mearsheimer, "Iran is Rushing to Build a Nuclear Weapon — and Trump Can't Stop It," *New York Times Online*, July 1, 2019, available at https://www.nytimes.com/2019/07/01/opinion/iran-is-rushing-to-build-a-nuclear-weapon-and-trump-cant-stop-it.html.

possibility of interstate war. If these can be ameliorated or eliminated reliably via systemic change, then eliminating nuclear weapons could be an easy, even natural consequence. If not, then at least some states will continue to seek nuclear weapons and, as a consequence, others will see a need to do so as well.

Realist thought does not contend that states should or will reject all forms of arms control — there may be occasion for agreement that is in each party's national interest. Indeed, the renowned Realist contributor to deterrence theory, the late Herman Kahn, while "not very hopeful" that "rule by law" could regulate international conflict, said that diplomatic efforts "are to be encouraged — in fact they are indispensable."[57] But in general, in an anarchic, self-help system states will *not* willingly part with those capabilities they consider *essential* to their security: "Simply stated, the world has yet to ban successfully any weapon deemed to be effective by those with the desire and the means to acquire it."[58] States will not willingly forego the capabilities they believe essential to their security on the hope or promise that cooperation will prevail and the threats they face will cease, or that their security needs will otherwise somehow be met. The prudent expectation must be that in a system that effectively remains lawless, a state's survival could, ultimately, be dependent on its own power. Such an expectation reasonably precludes a general willingness to forfeit necessary power in advance of the establishment of a reliable and enduring alternative security

---

[57] Herman Kahn, *The Nature and Feasibility of War and Deterrence*, 1888-RC (Santa Monica, CA: The RAND Corp., 1960), p. 45.

[58] Andrew Krepinevich, *US Nuclear Forces: Meeting the Challenge of a Proliferated World* (Washington, D.C.: Center for Strategic and Budgetary Assessments, 2009), p. 45.

mechanism that eliminates national security concerns, i.e., a new international political order.[59]

Reflecting this Realist logic, in 1929 President Herbert Hoover observed: "Until such time as nations can build the agencies of pacific settlement on stronger foundations; until fear, the most dangerous of all national emotions, has been proved groundless by long proof of international honesty; until the power of world public opinion as a restraint of aggression has had many years of test, there will not have been established that confidence which warrants the abandonment of preparedness for defense among nations. To do so may invite war."[60] This is the Realist's caution and lament.

Waltz's early Realist critique of the Idealist disarmament narrative reveals the divide separating Realism and Idealism, and its effect on views regarding nuclear disarmament. Waltz observes that there have been many past claims that a common fear stemming from the dangers of a new military technology — from lighter-than-air balloons to dynamite — would drive leaders to unprecedented cooperative action, effectively leaving the past behind. History demonstrates, however, that all such expectations have been dashed by reality.

The claim regarding the transformative effect of nuclear weapons, Waltz contends, will prove no more powerful a dynamic in this regard. This is not because the Russian, Chinese, or U.S. leaderships are foolish or ignorant, or because some national or international villain now

---

[59] Colin S. Gray, *House of Cards* (Ithaca, NY: Cornell University Press, 1992), p. 225. More recently, see Brad Roberts, "Ban the Bomb or Bomb the Ban? Next Steps on the Ban Treaty," European Leadership Network, *Global Security Policy Brief* (March 2018), pp. 1-9.

[60] Herbert Hoover, "Armistice Day Address," *Hoover.Archives.gov*, November 11, 1929, available at https://hoover.archives.gov/sites/default/files/research/ebooks/b2v1_full.pdf.

precluding disarmament must be corralled for disarmament to proceed. It is because different national leaderships predictably will perceive and respond differently to the lethality of nuclear weapons. It may inspire the "peace wish" of some, but not others: "One can equate fear with world peace only if the peace wish exists in all states and is uniformly expressed in their policies."[61] Different responses may be deemed reasonable and defensive national behavior in an anarchic system — depending on the external threat each state confronts or anticipates.

A tenet of much Realist thought emphasizes that the cooperative transformation of the international system to a benign order *is hardly plausible because the system lacks the mutual trust necessary for its own transformation.* To establish a much more cooperative system or a benevolent central authority with power would require a level of interstate trust that neither exists now nor *can exist prior* to the existence of a rule-based cooperative order that is reliably enforced — described by Professor Marion Boggs in 1941 as "a system of international law intolerant of violence...and an organization of the world community adequate to restrain hostilities."[62]

The Realist paradox that confronts the Idealist nuclear disarmament agenda is that international trust *must already exist* to enable the establishment of the central authority or cooperative system that could, in principle, mandate and enforce disarmament. Why so? Because in the absence of an existing high level of international trust, national leaders should not be expected to accept the risk of ceding their critical tools of power to a weak central authority such as today's United Nations. If they were to disarm prior to that central authority reliably providing collective security,

---

[61] Waltz, *Man, the State and War*, op. cit., pp. 235-236.

[62] Boggs, op. cit., pp. 102-104.

what then would provide for their protection if opponents did not simultaneously relinquish their tools of power? And, what authority and power would enforce their opponents' disarmament? The Realist asks: "Where would such a guarantee come from, and why would it be credible?"[63] States cannot prudently disarm simply trusting that others will cooperatively do likewise or that a central authority will one day emerge capable of protecting them and enforcing norms. If that level of cooperation and interstate trust existed reliably in the international system there would be no need for a central authority to provide order and enforce rules—cooperation would be the norm and could be expected. But as John Mearsheimer notes, "states can never be certain about other states' intentions....There is little room for trust among states."[64]

The lack of international trust is the condition that many Realists suggest permits "no exit" from the anarchic system. The ever-present prospect of aggression by untrustworthy states creates an inherent security concern for others, and the corresponding absence of international trust prevents the consensual creation of a central authority or cooperative order that transforms the system. Its creation would require all members to cooperate reliably and/or to transfer their power to the central authority near-simultaneously, trusting that possible adversaries would also do so. Yet, in the absence of an existing, overarching authority that itself is trustworthy and capable of enforcing good behavior, there can be no basis for expecting that all states would transfer power to a central authority, cooperate reliably, or establish a powerful decentralized cooperative interstate regime. During the celebration of the UN's 40th anniversary, then-UN General Undersecretary Brian Urquhart observed wryly that the international unity and cooperation needed

---

[63] Krepinevich, op. cit., p. 43.

[64] Mearsheimer, *The Tragedy of Great Power Politics*, op. cit., pp. 31-32.

to overcome systemic mistrust and anarchy will not be realized "until an invasion from Mars takes place."[65]

In sum, many Realists see a classic "chicken or egg" problem: the absence of adequate trust and cooperation in the international system drives the need for the transition to a reliable central authority or other cooperative order as envisaged by Idealists; but, it also undermines the potential for such a transition. As an assessment of the prospects for a cooperative transformation concludes: "Internationalist approaches tend to require as a precondition for success some degree of precisely what they seek to establish: a climate of international cooperation."[66]   Before prudent leaders will be willing to disarm, an alternative mechanism would need to provide national security.   Disarmament cannot be such a mechanism absent that element that does not exist in interstate relations and, by any empirical assessment, does not appear to be in sight, i.e., transformative mutual trust.

Consequently, Realists often conclude that it is a mistake to present nuclear disarmament as the enlightened alternative to nuclear deterrence and the risk of its failure. It is a non sequitur to assert that because nuclear war must be prevented, nuclear disarmament is the answer and thus nuclear deterrence should be abandoned. This is a false choice because whatever the weaknesses of nuclear deterrence, nuclear disarmament is not a plausible alternative; it essentially is *precluded* in any meaningful timeframe by the character of the international system and that system's lack of transformative interstate trust. Before leaders will be willing to disarm, national security would

---

[65] Quoted in George Spieker, Deutsche-Press Agentur, "Einigkeit in der UNO erst bei einer Invasion vom Mars," *Washington Journal*, July 5, 1985, p. 1.

[66] Welch, "Internationalism: Contacts, Trade, and Institutions," in *Fateful Visions: Avoiding Nuclear Catastrophe*, op. cit., p. 195.

need to be provided by an alternative mechanism; disarmament cannot be such a mechanism.

Realists then must ask the question, "how can we perpetuate peace without [first] solving the problem of war?" Nuclear deterrence is at least part of their answer: "although the possibility of war remains, nuclear weapons have drastically reduced the probability of its being fought by the states that have them."[67] Sir Lawrence Freedman of King's College London describes the dominance of this Realist conclusion during the Cold War: "If, as it seemed, there was no way of getting out of the nuclear age, then deterrence made the best of a bad job."[68]

While there is no Realist consensus on the level of confidence that may properly be attributed to deterrence strategies, Realists generally see value in nuclear deterrence to prevent war and its escalation from historical evidence. This conclusion regarding nuclear deterrence has been reached by a diverse set of academics, historians, and participant-observers.

For example, the late, distinguished deterrence theorist and academic, Bernard Brodie, concluded that "The Strategic nuclear forces of each of the superpowers do inhibit the other from any kind of warlike action against it. This was proved abundantly during the Cuban missile crisis..."[69] Similarly, from their meticulous research on U.S.-Soviet relations, Richard Lebow and Janice Stein conclude that nuclear deterrence moderated superpower behavior during the Cold War: "once leaders in Moscow and Washington recognized and acknowledged to the other

---

[67] Kenneth W. Waltz, "Nuclear Myths and Political Realists," *The American Political Science Review*, Vol. 84, No. 3 (September 1990), pp. 743-744.

[68] Lawrence Freedman, *Deterrence* (Malden, MA: Polity Press, 2004), p. 13.

[69] Bernard Brodie, "The Development of Nuclear Strategy," *International Security*, Vol. 2, No. 4 (Spring 1978), p. 76.

that a nuclear war between them would almost certainly lead to their mutual destruction....Fear of the consequences of nuclear war not only made it exceedingly improbable that either superpower would deliberately seek a military confrontation with the other; it made their leaders extremely reluctant to take any action that they considered would seriously raise the risk of war."[70] The renowned Cold War historian and Yale University professor, John Lewis Gaddis, similarly concludes that nuclear deterrence indeed contributed to the long peace among great powers since 1945, "a remarkable record, unparalleled in modern history," and that it is "likely to continue to be 'relevant' to the stability of the international system..."[71] And, based on a careful examination of Soviet Politburo records, Russian historian Victor Gobarev concludes that America's unique nuclear deterrence capabilities "counterbalanced" Soviet local conventional superiority and were "the single most important factor which restrained Stalin's possible temptation to resolve the [1948-1949] Berlin problem by military means. Evidence obtained from [Soviet] oral history clearly supports this fact."[72]

Evidence of the deterring effect of nuclear weapons is not limited to U.S.-Soviet Cold War history. Considerable available evidence indicates that Saddam Hussein was prevented from the use of chemical and biological weapons in 1991 by U.S. nuclear deterrence.[73] And, General Shankar

---

[70] Richard Ned Lebow and Janice Gross Stein, *We All Lost the Cold War* (Princeton, NJ: Princeton University Press), 1994, p. 367.

[71] John Lewis Gaddis, *The United States and the End of the Cold War* (Oxford: Oxford University Press, 1992), pp. 110, 118.

[72] Victor Gobarev, "Soviet Military Plans and Actions During the First Berlin Crisis, 1948-1949," *Journal of Slavic Military Studies*, Vol. 10, No. 3 (September 1997), p. 5; and James Acton, *Deterrence During Disarmament* (London: International Institute for Strategic Studies, March 2011), p. 34.

[73] Charles A. Duelfer, testimony, Senate Armed Services Committee, Subcommittee on Emerging Threats and Capabilities: The Weapons of

Roychowdhury, India's former Army Chief, has observed that, "Pakistan's nuclear weapons deterred India from attacking that country after the Mumbai strikes" and "it was due to Pakistan's possession of nuclear weapons that India stopped short of a military retaliation."[74] Historical evidence does *not* indicate that deterrence is infallible, but that nuclear weapons have contributed to the deterrence of war and escalation in the past.[75]

Thomas Schelling, one of the 20th century's most renowned deterrence theorists and a Nobel laureate, offered his observation regarding the nuclear disarmament narrative as popularized after the Cold War. His observation illustrates a Realist's skepticism and the basis for that skepticism, i.e., he pointed to the continuing value of nuclear deterrence in an anarchic system:

> Why should we expect a world without nuclear weapons to be safer than one with (some) nuclear weapons? ...I have not come across any mention of

Mass Destruction Program of Iraq, Senate Hearing 107-573, 107th Cong., 2nd Sess. (Washington, D.C.: GPO, 2002), pp. 92-93, at http://frwebgate.access.gpo.gov/cgibin/getdoc.cgi?dbname=107_senate_hearings&docid=f:80791.pdf. See also the work by Kevin Woods, task leader of the Iraqi Perspectives Project at the Institute for Defense Analyses, and David Palkki, deputy director of National Defense University's Conflict Records Research Center. They presented their respective views on this subject as described at a Policy Forum Luncheon by the Washington Institute for Near East Policy, "Knowing the Enemy: Iraqi Decisionmaking Under Saddam Hussein," September 20, 2010. This forum can be found at http://www.cspanarchives.org/program/id/233237.

[74] Quoted in, "Pak's N-bomb prevented Indian retaliation after 26/11," *The Indian Express*, March 9, 2009, available at http://www.indianexpress.com/news/paks-nbomb-prevented-indian-retaliation-after-2611/432730/0.

[75] See the discussion in Keith B. Payne and James Schlesinger, et al., *Minimum Deterrence: Examining the Evidence* (Fairfax, VA: National Institute Press, 2013), pp. 13-14.

what would happen in the event of a major war. One might hope that major war could not happen without nuclear weapons, but it always did....every responsible government must consider that other responsible governments will mobilize their nuclear weapons [production] base as soon as war erupts, or as soon as war appears likely, there will be at least covert frantic efforts, or perhaps purposely conspicuous efforts to acquire deliverable nuclear weapons as rapidly as possible.   And what then?...The [existing] nuclear quiet should not be traded away for a world in which a brief race to reacquire nuclear weapons could become every former nuclear state's overriding preoccupation.[76]

As Schelling's comment suggests, many Realists consider a "nuclear world" in which deterrence is the policy guide to be safer than a nuclear-disarmed world. Bernard Brodie concludes: "...nuclear weapons do act critically to deter war between major powers, and not nuclear wars alone but any wars. That is really a very great gain. We should no doubt be hesitant about relinquishing it even if we could."[77]   Waltz elaborates on the rationale for this conclusion: "[Nuclear weapons] make the cost of war seem frighteningly high and thus discourage states from starting any wars that might lead to the use of such weapons. Nuclear weapons have helped maintain peace between the great powers and have not led their few other possessors to

---

[76] Thomas Schelling, "A World Without Nuclear Weapons?," *Daedalus* (Fall 2009), pp. 125-126, 129. Decades earlier, Schelling indicated his preference — in contrast to what he called "the 'ban the bomb' orientation" — is for deterrence to be viewed, "as something to be enhanced, not dismantled." See Thomas Schelling, *The Strategy of Conflict* (Cambridge, MA: Harvard University Press, 1960), p. 241.

[77] Bernard Brodie, *War and Politics* (New York: Macmillan, 1973), p. 430.

military adventures....Wars become less likely as the costs of war rise in relation to possible gain."[78] The great contribution of nuclear weapons to peace and stability is that, when properly deployed, they can preclude a would-be aggressor's expectation of gain. And, if conflict occurs, the presence of nuclear weapons can limit its likely escalation.[79] Indeed, Waltz contends that the disarmament narrative's emphasis on the destructive consequences of nuclear war "has obscured the important benefits [nuclear weapons] promise to states trying to coexist in a self-help world,"[80] and that nuclear disarmament, in addition to being "fanciful," would "deny the peaceful benefits of nuclear weapons to those [states] who need them."[81]

A recent editorial discussing British nuclear weapons appearing in *The Times* of London captures this Realist position concisely: "Britain's nuclear arsenal is periodically a matter of political controversy but no responsible government would lightly give up a deterrent. In an anarchic international order, the risks of abandoning it would be incalculable."[82] And, as former British Prime Minister Margaret Thatcher similarly explained years earlier: "Wars are not caused by the buildup of weapons. They are caused when an aggressor believes he can achieve objectives at an acceptable price....Our task is to see that potential aggressors, from whatever quarter, understand plainly that the capacity and resolve of the West would

---

[78] Waltz, "The Spread of Nuclear Weapons: More May be Better," op. cit.

[79] Ibid.

[80] Ibid.

[81] In Scott Sagan and Kenneth N. Waltz, *The Spread of Nuclear Weapons: A Debate Renewed* (New York: Norton and Co., 2003), p. 152.

[82] "Deterrence Defended," *The Times* (UK), May 3, 2019, available at https://www.thetimes.co.uk/article/the-times-view-on-the-trident-service-at-westminster-abbey-deterrence-defended-2pn9vx6zx.

deny them victory and that the price they would pay would be intolerable."[83]

Conflicting Philosophies and Conflicting Definitions of Reasonable and Responsible

The key point here is that the fundamental difference separating the contending narratives on nuclear disarmament often reflects their very different interrelated conceptions of the international system, the potential for a cooperative transformation of the existing anarchic international system, and, correspondingly, the value of nuclear deterrence.   These differing philosophical foundations underlie competing conclusions about the feasibility of global nuclear disarmament and the prudence of pursuing it as the priority goal.

E.H. Carr offered an explanation of the fundamental differences between Realists and Idealists ("Utopians" in Carr's terms) and the all-encompassing effect of those differences: "The two methods of approach — the [Idealist] inclination to ignore what was and what is in contemplation of *what should be,* and the [Realist] inclination to deduce what should be from *what was and what is* — determine opposite attitudes towards every political problem."[84]

---

[83] Quoted in, Keith Payne, *The Great American Gamble* (Fairfax, VA: National Institute Press, 2008), p. 149. The former socialist French president, François Hollande made much the same point: "The international context does not allow any weaknesses…the era of nuclear deterrence is therefore not over… In a dangerous world — and it is dangerous — France does not want to let down its guard…" Quoted in "'Dangerous World:' France Has Less Than 300 Nukes and Still Needs Them," *Reuters*, February 20, 2015, available at http://rt.com/news/234099-france-details-nuclear-arsenal/.

[84] Carr, op. cit., p. 11. (Emphasis added).

These differences are displayed in contending narratives regarding nuclear disarmament.

These narratives involve different expectations about human decision-making and what is and is not possible with regard to the structure of the international system. Seeing the evidence of history and enduring patterns of human behavior, Realists contend that the needed timely transformation of the international system to enable nuclear disarmament is not plausible. The Realists' skepticism is based not on malevolence, but on the inescapable constraints that an anarchic system places on prudent leadership: If some national leaders continue to deem nuclear weapons necessary for their state's security — and thus will not part with them — others will be compelled to do likewise.[85]

In contrast, the Idealist disarmament narrative posits that the future can be fundamentally different as reason and the global threat of nuclear weapons compel leaders and peoples toward unprecedented cooperative steps and the transformation of the international system.   It is not thoughtless sentimentalism; it sees nuclear disarmament as both a possible dynamic for that transition process and a consequence of it.

These Realists and Idealists consequently bring different speculative assumptions to the question and see fundamentally different goals and actions as reasonable for national decision-making: Realists see national leaders as continually compelled by security concerns to pursue state

---

[85] As Clinton Administration Under Secretary of Defense for Policy Walter Slocombe observed in 1997, "There is no reasonable prospect that all the declared and de facto nuclear powers will agree in the near term to give up all their nuclear weapons. And as long as one such state refuses to do so, it will be necessary for us to retain a nuclear force of our own." Senate Governmental Affairs Committee, Subcommittee on International Security, Proliferation and Federal Services, *Statement of the Honorable Walter B. Slocombe, Undersecretary of Defense for Policy, Hearing on Nuclear Weapons and Deterrence*, February 12, 1997, p. 7.

power, potentially including nuclear power, as prudent and necessary to mitigate those concerns. Idealists see the continuing national accumulation of power, particularly including nuclear power, as the greatest security threat confronting all humankind. They thus seek to marshal global popular and elite opinion in opposition to nuclear weapons in the expectation that general nuclear disarmament is feasible and necessary for global security. These fundamentally conflicting Realist and Idealist perspectives about 1) the character of the international system, 2) the source of greatest risk to states in the system, and, 3) what constitutes prudent, reasonable behavior for national leaders, drive incompatible conclusions about the wisdom and feasibility of global nuclear disarmament and the relative value of nuclear deterrence.

The Continuing Power of Mistrust

In an apparent confirmation of Realist claims about the continuing power of the international system's anarchic nature and lack of trust to shape national policies, neither Russia nor China followed the U.S. lead of the past decade promoting "nuclear zero."[86] The problem for them, as Paul Bracken has observed, was that, "Nuclear abolition — as seen from Moscow, Beijing, Pyongyang — looked like a way to make the world safe for U.S. conventional strong-arm tactics."[87]

Jon Wolfsthal, a senior official with responsibility for arms control during the Obama Administration, acknowledged that Moscow's mistrust of a powerful United

---

[86] The Chinese Foreign Minister, Wang Yi, recently affirmed that China "has no interest" in negotiating a nuclear arms control treaty with the United States and Russia. See "China 'has no interest' in joining US-Russia nuclear deal," *Associated Press*, May 13, 2019, available at https://www.apnews.com/50c0fb070533401fab1143d61e0cdb21.

[87] Bracken, op. cit.

States undermined its possible interest in nuclear disarmament: "…every time we said we wanted to reduce the role of nuclear weapons…what Russia heard was, we want to be able to do whatever we want with conventional weapons anytime, anywhere."[88] Indeed, President Putin reportedly viewed the U.S. proposal for nuclear zero "as just another U.S. trick to weaken his country."[89] Correspondingly, Alexei Arbatov, a well-known Russian national security expert and former senior member of the Russian Duma, identifies the basic problems in U.S.-Russian relations in Realist terms, "political hostilities, intransigence and *total distrust*."[90]

The Deputy Commander of U.S. Strategic Command, Vice Admiral David Kriete, concludes that following the Cold War,

> One of the assumptions made [in 2010] was that Russia is our friend, and if the United States leads the world in reducing the roles of numbers of nuclear weapons, and their prominence in our national security policies, then the rest of the world would follow. It's a very noble goal. But the intervening eight years proved to be very difficult because every other country that has nuclear weapons that could potentially threaten the United States or our allies did exactly the opposite. While

---

[88] Quoted in, *Press Briefing: The Trump Administration's New Nuclear Posture Review*, Carnegie Endowment for International Peace, January 23, 2018, at https://wwwarmscontrol.org/taxonomy/term/4.

[89] Quoted in, "Reviving Nuclear Arms Talks," December 15, 2008, available at http://gm5-lkweb.newscyclecloud.com/news/20081215/reviving-nuclear-arms-talks.

[90] Quoted in Peter Cobus, "Analysts Call Scrapping INF 'Strategic Catastrophe' for Kremlin," *VOA News*, February 2, 2019, available at https://www.voanews.com/a/analysts-call-scrapping-inf-strategic-catastrophe-for-kremlin/4770067.html. (Emphasis added).

the United States actually did reduce the numbers and some of the types of [nuclear] systems, Russia greatly increased their number of nuclear weapons, the means that they have to deliver them, and most importantly, the prominence that nuclear weapons play in their military doctrine...we saw China increase their number of nuclear weapons, and...North Korea developed not only a nuclear weapons capability, but also, throughout 2017 and 2018, a whole number of ballistic missile launchers of various ranges.[91]

The Director of the Defense Intelligence Agency, Lt. Gen. Robert Ashley, remarked that: "Russia sees its nuclear weapons as the ultimate guarantor of the country's survival, perceives a warfighting role for [their] use, and directs its scarce resources to its nuclear modernization effort... China is likely to double the size of its nuclear stockpile in the course of implementing the most rapid expansion and diversification of its nuclear arsenal in China's history."[92]

Russian leaders clearly continue to see nuclear weapons as essential to Russia's security and are unwilling to forego them in a dangerous world. American General Curtis Scaparrotti, NATO's Supreme Allied Commander, observed that Russia values and modernizes its nuclear weapons arsenal as the means necessary to succeed against

---

[91] Quoted in, Maria Gallucci, "How the United States Plans to Update its Nuclear Arsenal," *IEEE Spectrum*, May 20, 2019, available at https://spectrum.ieee.org/energywise/aerospace/military/a-qa-with-us-nuclear-weapons-expert.

[92] Remarks by Lt. Gen. Robert P. Ashley, Jr., Director, Defense Intelligence Agency, "Russian and Chinese Nuclear Modernization Trends," May 29, 2019, available at https://www.dia.mil/News/Speeches-and-Testimonies/Article-View/Article/1859890/russian-and-chinese-nuclear-modernization-trends/.

the United States: "…it facilitates Moscow's mistaken belief that limited nuclear first use, potentially including low-yield [nuclear] weapons, can provide Russia a coercive advantage in crises and at lower levels of conflict."[93]

Andrei Kokoshin, a member of the Russian State Duma and former Russian Security Council Secretary, observed in 2010, "There will be no alternative to nuclear deterrence even in the distant future."[94] Russian commentator, Mikhail Alexandrov, captured apparent thinking in Moscow: "Given NATO's clear advantage in conventional armaments, the threat of a nuclear response currently serves as Russia's main deterrent against aggression."[95] Apparently in response to expressed U.S. interest in the possibility of further nuclear reductions, the head of the Russian Duma's Committee on International Affairs, Leonid Slutsky, stated, "Balance of powers between Moscow and Washington is based on so-called mutual assured destruction. If it won't be the case anymore, there

---

[93] Quoted in Joel Gehrke, "Russians Are Serious About Using Nukes, US NATO General Warns," *Washington Examiner*, March 13, 2019, at https://www.washingtonexaminer.com/policy/defense-national-security/russians-are-serious-about-using-nukes-us-nato-general-warns. The Commander of U.S. Strategic Command, Charles Richard, says similarly, "Russian military doctrine emphasizes the potential coercive and military uses of nuclear weapons and Russia fields advanced capabilities to achieve these objectives. Moreover, Russian doctrine and rhetoric highlights a willingness to use nuclear weapons first, perhaps in an attempt to terminate a conventional conflict on terms acceptable to Russia." See, Admiral Charles Richard, *Statement of Charles A. Richard, Commander of United States Strategic Command Before the Senate Committee on Armed Services*, February 13, 2020, pp. 4-5.

[94] Kokoshin quoted in, "No Alternative to Nuclear Deterrence," *Interfax-AVN Online*, November 22, 2010, at http://www.dialog.com/proquestdialog/.

[95] Quoted in, "Good Luck With That: Obama Tries to Trick Russia Into Nuclear Disarmament," *Sputnik News*, July 12, 2016, at http://sputniknews.com/politics/20160712/1042856945/us-new-start-proposal-folly.html.

would be a risk of real war, no more, no less."[96] Correspondingly, Russia's Ambassador to the United States, Anatoly Antonov, has emphasized that Russia has no interest in an agreement to limit its new types of nuclear weapons,[97] and labeled as "impossible" and "useless" attempts to seek the disarmament of nuclear powers "in defiance of their legitimate security interests."[98]   Even during the early post-Cold War euphoria in U.S.-Russian relations, Alexei Arbatov observed that, "the only abiding guarantee of safety is one's own nuclear deterrent potential.... Mutual deterrence is the best scenario for strategic relations" because "no more attractive substitute has been conceived despite the sea of rhetoric and the embraces and toasts..."[99]

A final illustration of pertinent contemporary Russian thinking is from a recent Russian report sponsored by the Foreign Ministry and the State Duma, *The New Understanding and Ways to Strengthen Multilateral Strategic Stability*. Referring to "multilateral strategic stability," the report contends that, "Its underlying factor is still deterrence which is based on a potential aggressor's awareness of unavoidable punishment and guaranteed ability of the victim of aggression to inflict unacceptable damage upon the aggressor in a second strike.... *This automatically excludes nuclear disarmament.*" The report adds

---

[96] Romeo Ranoco, "Nuclear Disarmament of Russia, US and China Could Lead to Real War — Russian MP," *Reuters*, April 26, 2019.

[97] Patrick Tucker, "New New START a Nonstarter: Russian Ambassador," *DefenseOne.com*, March 12, 2019, at https:///.defenseone.com/politics/2019/03/new-new-start-nonstarter-russian-ambassador/155474/print/.

[98] "Moscow Will Not Support Full Nuclear Disarmament — Russia's US Ambassador," December 1, 2017, *TASS.com*, at http://tass.com/politics/978523.

[99] Alexei Arbatov, "Once More on Missile Defense: Is Stability Formula Attainable?" *Moscow Nezavisimaya Gazeta*, July 4, 2001 (Foreign Broadcast Information Service translated text).

that Russian acquisition of multiple new strategic nuclear systems is a, "positive element of the military-strategic environment of huge importance," and that these new Russian nuclear systems "objectively curb the arms race."[100]

The consequences of mistrust—seemingly inherent in the anarchic interstate system—are predictable. Given Moscow's perception of threats to its security, distrust of the United States, and no prospect in sight of a reliable global authority or cooperative interstate system, Russian leaders are unwilling to give up nuclear weapons: "Russia's deterrence potential should be ensured by an efficient modernization of Russia's strategic [nuclear] forces, not by any formal guarantees from the U.S."[101] This does not necessarily reflect malevolence on Moscow's part; Russian leaders undoubtedly see no prudent option for nuclear disarmament. Even if others plead benign intentions, intentions can change. Such concerns are the natural consequence of an anarchic system. As Waltz observes, "In international politics...friendliness and hostility are transient qualities."[102]

Realism and Idealism in U.S. Nuclear Policy

While the philosophic divide separating Realists and Idealists is substantial, there can be a convergence of policy views across this divide. For example, for a relatively brief period following the peaceful conclusion of the Cold War and amid widespread, optimistic expectations of a "New World Order," nuclear disarmament rebounded as a

---

[100] Sergei Karaganov and Dmitry Suslov, *The New Understanding and Ways to Strengthen Multilateral Strategic Stability* (Moscow: Higher School of Economics, National Research University, 2019), pp. 6, 28. (Emphasis added).

[101] Alexei Arbatov, "The Twists and Turns of Missile Defense," *Nezavisimaya Gazeta*, November 7, 2011, available at eastview.com.

[102] Waltz, *The Spread of Nuclear Weapons: More May be Better*, op. cit.

contender for U.S. nuclear policy dominance. Some prominent Realists adopted the nuclear disarmament agenda—if not the underlying Idealist philosophic positions. Indeed, it must be noted that not all disarmament proponents are necessarily Idealists. Four prominent former U.S. senior officials with extensive national security experience joined to advocate for nuclear disarmament: George Shultz, William Perry, Henry Kissinger, and Sam Nunn.[103] The advocacy of nuclear disarmament by former senior officials, particularly including former Secretary of State Henry Kissinger, illustrated that some prominent figures with undoubted Realist credentials adopted the goals of the contemporary disarmament narrative.

For Realists, acceptance of the "nuclear zero" goal appeared to be based largely on several popular Western post-Cold War notions: 1) the collapse of the Soviet Union and relatively benign relations with Russia and China immediately following the Cold War had largely eliminated any serious interstate nuclear threats for the West;[104] 2) nuclear terrorism was now the serious potential nuclear threat, and counterproliferation measures—*not* nuclear

---

[103] See for example, George P. Shultz, William J. Perry, Henry A. Kissinger, and Sam Nunn, "A World Free of Nuclear Weapons," *The Wall Street Journal*, January 4, 2007, at https://www.wsj.com/articles/SB116787515251566636; and George P. Shultz, William J. Perry, Henry A. Kissinger, and Sam Nunn, "Toward a Nuclear-Free World," *The Wall Street Journal*, January 15, 2008, at https://www.wsj.com/articles/SB120036422673589947.

[104] In 1995, then-Secretary of Defense William Perry observed that, "Today, Russia is a partner rather than an enemy." *Annual Report to the President and the Congress* (Washington, D.C.: Department of Defense, February 1995), p. 8. In 2010, Secretary of Defense Robert Gates said that, "I don't see Russia as a threat. I see Russia—Russian-U.S. relations being those of normal states now." Interfax News Agency Interview with Secretary Gates, *News Transcript*, U.S. Department of Defense, September 13, 2010, at http://www.defense.gov/Transcripts/Transcript.aspx?TranscriptID=4687.

deterrence — were key to addressing that threat; and, 3) U.S. conventional force superiority around the globe allowed the United States to meet its priority security needs *without the need for nuclear weapons*.[105]

The apparent Realist evolution in favor of nuclear disarmament, however, arose and subsided relatively quickly. As great power relations in the post-Cold War era moved rapidly and unexpectedly in hostile directions, most Realist support for the "Nuclear Zero Campaign" appeared to wane. Realists generally did not believe the transformation of the international system to be forthcoming such that Western security concerns would be addressed by some form of global cooperative or collective security. Rather, for Realists, support for nuclear zero was based on the popular view that in the post-Cold War era, nuclear weapons were increasingly irrelevant to U.S. national security within a much-changed security context. For the United States, security challenges remained, but because the U.S. power position was so overwhelming *without nuclear weapons*, the United States could meet them without nuclear capabilities: "In a non-nuclear world, America would enjoy the advantages of geography (the protection afforded by two wide oceans and friendly neighbors in Canada and Mexico), the world's most powerful conventional forces, and an unrivaled network of

---

[105] Each of these points is well-reflected in, James Cartwright, Bruce Blair, et al., *Modernizing U.S. Nuclear Strategy, Force Structure and Posture, Global Zero US Nuclear Policy Commission Report* (Washington, D.C.: Global Zero, May 2012), at http://www.globalzero.org/files/ gz_us_nuclear_policy_commission_ report.pdf. Many proponents have suggested that nuclear disarmament should be attractive to the United States because it, "can gain from its strong comparative advantage in conventional technologies..." See, Cortright and Väyrynen, op. cit., p. 19.

allies."[106] Some Realists thus could conclude that the United States was well-positioned to forego nuclear weapons.

Consequently, Realists supporting the disarmament agenda had not necessarily embraced Idealist thought, per se. Instead, they were able to endorse nuclear disarmament for reasons well within the Realist philosophic tradition:[107] as the globe's only "hyperpower," the United States could prudently dispense with nuclear weapons without undermining its own security position.   With this construction, some Realists could lend their voices in favor of nuclear disarmament.   Interestingly, *the American conventional force advantages that gave some U.S. Realists the freedom to endorse nuclear disarmament had precisely the opposite effect on Russian Realists* — reflecting again the power of the anarchic structure of the international system to shape national thinking.

The re-emergence of great power hostilities and nuclear threats appeared to cool much continuing enthusiasm for the nuclear disarmament agenda among American Realists, especially those with national security responsibilities.[108]

---

[106] Steven Pifer, "10 Years after Obama's Nuclear-Free Vision, the US and Russia head in the Opposite Direction," April 4, 2019, at https://www.brookings.edu/blog/order-from-chaos/2019/04/04/10-years-after-obamas-nuclear-free-vision-the-us-and-russia-head-in-the-opposite-direction. This contention that global nuclear disarmament would be of unique advantage to the United States because of U.S. non-nuclear capabilities is not new. Former Secretary of Defense Les Aspin made the same point in 1992. For the United States, "A world without nuclear weapons would be better," because "The United States is the biggest conventional power in the world." See, Les Aspin, "Three Propositions for a New Era Nuclear Policy," *MIT News*, June 3, 1992, available at http://news.mit.edu/1992/propositions-0603.

[107] This point that Realist support for the "nuclear zero" agenda emerged *without* the acceptance of Idealist thinking was rightly noted by Richard Falk. See, David Krieger and Richard Falk, "Where We Stand: A Dialogue," in, *At the Nuclear Precipice*, op. cit., pp. 236, 245.

[108] See for example, Henry Kissinger and Brent Scowcroft, "Nuclear Weapons Reductions Must Be Part of Strategic Analysis," *Washington*

As Frank Rose, the Obama Administration's Assistant Secretary of State for Arms Control, observed in support of a comprehensive U.S. nuclear modernization program: "The security environment has changed dramatically since President Barack Obama delivered his famous speech in Prague in April 2009. Instead of joining the United States in expanding efforts to reduce nuclear threats, Russia and China have gone in the opposite direction, investing in new nuclear weapons systems, conventional strike, and asymmetric capabilities....Given these realities, it is critical that the United States modernize its strategic nuclear deterrent in a way that reassures allies and enhances strategic stability."[109]

The tension between Realism and Idealism in U.S. foreign policy can be traced to the country's founding.[110] To a considerable extent, however, there has been a Realist consistency in U.S. nuclear policy for decades.[111]

Post, April 22, 2012. The most recent joint article regarding nuclear weapons by three of the original "four horsemen" focuses not on "nuclear zero," but on "meaningful dialogue between Washington and Moscow," increasing "cooperation, transparency, and security," "strengthening the North Atlantic Treaty Organization and renewing dialogue with Russia," and "dialogue on strategic stability." These are all recommendations that Realists can applaud. See, George Shultz, William J. Perry, and Sam Nunn, "The Threat of Nuclear War is Still With Us," *The Wall Street Journal*, April 11, 2019, p. A17.

[109] Frank Rose and Benjamin Bahney, "Reassuring Allies and Strengthening Strategic Stability: An Approach to Nuclear Modernization for Democrats," *War on the Rocks*, April 16, 2019, at https://warontherocks.com/2019/04/reassuring-allies-and-strengthening-strategic-stability-an-approach-to-nuclear-modernization-for-democrats.

[110] See, Bernard Bailyn, *To Begin the World Anew* (New York: Vintage Books, 2003), pp. 60-99.

[111] See Kurt Guthe, *Ten Continuities in U.S. Nuclear Weapons Policy, Strategy, Plans, and Forces* (Fairfax, VA: National Institute Press, September 2008), available at http://www.nipp.org/wp-content/uploads/2014/11/N-Continuities-Draft_Rev-2.11.pdf.

Throughout the Cold War, as now, the global threat of nuclear weapons clearly animated an Idealist disarmament orientation in much of the academic and popular commentary regarding nuclear weapons. But with a few, brief exceptions, Republican and Democratic administration officials have brought Realist thought to the U.S. nuclear policy table. The manifest nuclear threat to the United States and allies posed by the Soviet Union during the Cold War undoubtedly encouraged *official* thinking toward Realism, but much less so academic thinking.

The late Sir Michael Howard helped to explain why: "Nobody who has been brought into contact with that inner group of civil and military specialists who are responsible for the security of this country can fail to notice the almost physical pressure exerted on them by that responsibility, affecting their processes of thought (and often their manner of speech) in much the same way as the movements of a man are affected when he tries to walk in water....they share a common skepticism as to the possibility of disarmament, or indeed of the creation of any effective international authority to whom they can turn over any portion of their responsibilities." Sir Michael adds the critical point that, "the impatient onlookers, who have never themselves been plunged into that element, cannot understand why."[112]

In an apparent official U.S. embrace of an Idealist agenda for nuclear disarmament, the 1968 Non-Proliferation Treaty, a treaty to which the United States is fully committed, calls on each party, "to pursue negotiations in good faith on effective measures relating to cessation of the nuclear arms race at an early date and to nuclear disarmament..." However, immediately following that text language in Article VI is the following proviso:

---

[112] Howard, op. cit., pp. 215-216.

"...and on a Treaty on general and complete disarmament under strict and effective international control."

Even the most dowdy Realist can embrace the call for nuclear disarmament in the context of "general and complete disarmament under strict and effective international control." How so? The condition of "general and complete disarmament under strict and effective international control" must presume that the international order has been transformed and that a reliable form of global collective security has been established — effectively mitigating the interstate security dilemma. With the assumption of such a transformed international order, Realists can easily support nuclear disarmament — even while doubting that such an order is ever likely to be established — because security concerns and interstate armed conflict would no longer be an enduring feature of the international system. Perhaps this is why a 1969 National Security Council analysis of the Non-Proliferation Treaty for then-National Security Advisor Henry Kissinger states that the Treaty's commitment to nuclear disarmament "is an essentially hortatory statement and presents no problems."[113]

President Obama's famed 2009 Prague speech emphasizing nuclear disarmament also suggested an official embrace of an Idealist nuclear disarmament agenda: "The United States will take concrete steps towards a world without nuclear weapons." However, President Obama's endorsement of nuclear zero was followed immediately by a Realist caveat: "Make no mistake: As long as these [nuclear] weapons exist, the United States will maintain a safe, secure and effective arsenal to deter any adversary, and guarantee that defense to our allies..." Similarly, the

---

[113] Spurgeon Keeny, *Memorandum For Dr. Kissinger, Provisions of the NPT and Associated Problems*, The White House, January 24, 1969, Declassified August 6, 2007, p. 5, available at https://2001-2009.state.gov/documents/organization/90727.pdf.

Obama Administration's 2010 *Nuclear Posture Review* identified nuclear disarmament as a top U.S. priority, but also emphasized the point that the "very demanding" international conditions necessary for disarmament "do not exist today."[114]

For those officials responsible for national security, global concepts based on the expectation of unprecedented and near-universal consensus and cooperation are likely to appear very distant and fragile given the external threats they must confront. As Michael Howard explained, the burden of security responsibility hangs heavily. Reflecting this dynamic and its implications for official thinking about deterrence and nuclear weapons, Lisa Gordon-Hagerty, Under Secretary for Nuclear Security at the U.S. Department of Energy recently observed:

> Despite the aspiration of a world without nuclear weapons, we must take the world as it is, not as we wish it were. Potential peer competitors such as Russia and China are investing massive resources into upgrading and expanding their nuclear arsenals, while regional adversaries such as North Korea and Iran defy the international community's decrees regarding their nuclear and missile programs. Worse, these states have made clear that nuclear weapons will be a vital element of their statecraft as they threaten U.S. interests around the world.[115]

---

[114] Department of Defense, *Nuclear Posture Review Report* (April 2010), p. xv.

[115] Lisa Gordon-Hagerty, "Modernizing Our Nuclear Enterprise Infrastructure to Keep Americans Safe," *The Oak Ridger* (Oak Ridge, Tennessee), February 7, 2020, available at https://www.oakridger.com/news/20200207/modernizing-our-nuclear-enterprise-infrastructure-to-keep-americans-safe.

Air Force Chief of Staff General David Goldfein similarly stated, "I would never advocate to place ourselves in a position where we might give up our [nuclear] second-strike capability... causing a potential change in enemy calculus.... Our nuclear deterrent underwrites American freedom and prosperity in both competition and war."[116] Or, as one Air Force General Officer quipped regarding the prospect of nuclear disarmament, "I hope that day comes. I hope that day comes soon. And when it does, I want to invite you all over to my house for a party. I'd just ask that you don't feed any of the hors d'oeuvres to my unicorn."[117]

Realism and Idealism: Reasoned Dialogue, Debate and Reconciliation?

There are numerous consequences of the connections between Realist and Idealist thought and contending nuclear narratives. Perhaps the most obvious is its effect on the character of the internal U.S. debate about nuclear disarmament. Idealist nuclear disarmament advocates and their Realist skeptics seem to talk past each other, including in academic settings.[118] As the renowned British academic

---

[116] Charles Pope, "Goldfein Offers Rationale for Nuclear Modernization and 'Failsafe' Deterrent," *Air Force News Service*, June 26, 2019, available at https://www.af.mil/News/Article-Display/Article/1888594/goldfein-offers-rationale-for-nuclear-modernization-and-failsafe-deterrence/.

[117] Quoted in, Keith B. Payne and James Schlesinger, et al., *Minimum Deterrence: Examining the Evidence*, op. cit., p. 3.

[118] Hugh Gusterson, "The dangerous disregard of nuclear experts for one another," *Bulletin of the Atomic Scientists*, March 25, 2015, available at https://thebulletin.org/2015/03/the-dangerous-disregard-of-nuclear-experts-for-one-another/. Johns Hopkins Professor Francis Gavin rightly notes, "The nuclear field...seems especially divided and stovepiped into various tribes. Nuclear policy is discussed in fundamentally different ways in different settings." See, "We Need to Talk: The Past, Present and Future of U.S. Nuclear Weapons Policy,"

Colin Gray noted in this regard 35 years ago, "a close observer of the U.S. defense debate of the past ten years could not help but notice the doctrinal rigidity that has characterized different schools of [nuclear policy] thought... All too frequently, policy debaters choose not to hear the arguments of the other side."[119] The notion that "iron sharpens iron,"[120] i.e., that each side can learn from the other, appears to have been lost. Instead, a result of this seemingly irreconcilable divide is that nuclear Idealists and Realists typically engage within their own closed circles and echo chambers. Two mutually exclusive positions are expressed vocally and repetitively, with little reference to the other except as a foil against which to argue. As in the past, Idealists advance a global solution to a critical concern, that concern now being the existence of nuclear weapons; Realists often respond with great skepticism regarding the feasibility—and thus the wisdom—of an Idealist global solution. As in the past, Idealists counter that their solution "must be made to work because the consequences of its failure to work would be so disastrous."[121] Technology advances, but this familiar Realist and Idealist juxtaposition remains unchanged.

Instead, these contending Realist and Idealist narratives often portray each other as contributing to the respective security threats that concern them most. Indeed, the occasionally expressed disdain each side has for the other—built on seemingly irreconcilable differences—can be palpable. In a relatively small policy community, this gulf appears to have long cooled much enthusiasm for reasoned,

War on the Rocks, January 2, 2017, available at, https://warontherocks.com/2017/01/we-need-to-talk-the-past-present-and-future-of-u-s-nuclear-weapons-policy/.

[119] Colin S. Gray, *Nuclear Strategy and Strategic Planning* (Philadelphia: Foreign Policy Research Institute, 1984), pp. 55, 59.

[120] From Proverbs 27:17.

[121] Carr, op. cit., p. 8.

amicable discourse. Idealists often appear to see Realists as acting from bad or foolish intent to prevent reasonable and prudent movement toward global transformation and nuclear disarmament.[122]   Some seem to doubt even the possibility of principled, thoughtful Realist opposition to their disarmament agenda and deem Realists who are critical as being hard-headed, hard-hearted, or psychologically deficient.   How else to explain Realist skepticism of the obviously unalloyed moral good of pursuing global transformation and nuclear disarmament as the priority goal?   Realists see a continuing security concern, and thus often appear to consider Idealist disarmament initiatives as naïvely threatening U.S. deterrence capabilities and security in a dangerous and anarchic international environment.   They threaten the "comfort" that Waltz contends resides in "the fact that history has shown that where nuclear capabilities emerge, so, too, does stability."[123]

Each side can view the other as being an obstacle to decisions and actions that are obviously prudent and necessary to preserve security — *with many Idealists advocating from a global perspective for changed national behavior, and many Realists seeking instead to preserve national power given the continuing insecurity of global anarchy.* Their differences following from their conflicting philosophical moorings are portrayed in Figure 1 below. They appear largely irreconcilable, allowing little margin for a possible "middle ground." But that appearance could give way — to some extent — to sincere, civil efforts to find a synthesis.

---

[122] For a classic example of this Idealist thinking see, Walter Cronkite, "Cronkite Champions World Government," *The Washington Times*, December 3, 1999, p. A2.

[123] Kenneth Waltz, "Why Iran Should Get the Bomb," *Foreign Affairs*, Vol. 91, No. 4 (July-August 2012), p. 5.

Figure 1. A Simplified Comparison of Realist and Idealist Thought as Applied to Nuclear Policy

REALIST THOUGHT	IDEALIST THOUGHT
The international system is anarchic; deterrence is needed to prevent attacks: Maintain nuclear weapons.	The international system is anarchic; nuclear weapons and deterrence imperil all humanity: Eliminate for global survival.
Insufficient international trust exists for timely global systemic change. Mistrust in the anarchic system is prudent and reasonable.	Sufficient international trust and cooperation can and must be established for system transformation and disarmament.
The international system must be transformed *before* disarmament is possible.	Disarmament can spur further international systemic transformation.
In the absence of reliable global collective security, disarmament cannot be expected. Some states will maintain nuclear weapons, judging it is reasonable and prudent to do so for national survival.	Unprecedented cooperation is possible. States should willingly forego nuclear weapons; the global risk they pose makes it prudent and reasonable to do so.
A common global interest sufficient to overcome mistrust does not appear to exist.	A common global interest sufficient to mitigate mistrust is to eliminate nuclear weapons.
Basic patterns of international behavior have not changed; policies should not be predicated on the expectation of timely change.	Basic patterns of leadership decision-making and international behavior can change with the application of reason and enlightened self-interest.
Idealist disarmament policy recommendations are naïve at best and potentially contrary to national security requirements.	Realist thought is deficient and an obstacle to needed global progress and disarmament.

Summary and Conclusions

Realism and Idealism posit contrary basic beliefs about human decision-making and the character of interstate relations. Referencing history, Realists tend to focus on the constraints that an anarchic international system and established patterns of human decision-making place on interstate behavior—compelling national leaders to prioritize power in response to the security threats inherent in an anarchic system. In contrast, Idealists see the dangers of an anarchic system and focus on the priority goal of transforming it—a goal they deem feasible if national leaders will follow reason and enlightened self-interest. These contrary Realist and Idealist starting points lead to very different conclusions about what constitute reasonable national goals and prudent behavior.

Applied to nuclear policy, Idealist thought for decades has been the basis for a series of largely academic proposals for the transformation of international relations and nuclear disarmament. U.S. Cold War declarations about nuclear policy often reflected Idealist aspirations, but U.S. maintenance of a powerful nuclear arsenal generally reflected persistent Realist thought.

Proponents of nuclear disarmament now often contend that the elimination of nuclear weapons is an immediate imperative for human survival and seek a cooperative transition of the international system that enables disarmament—as Idealists envisage. Some dismiss strategies of nuclear deterrence as an ill-fated and foolish rationale for nuclear weapons that undermines their efforts to "stigmatize" nuclear weapons and establish a powerful global norm against them. Consequently, proponents of nuclear disarmament tend to elevate global transformation and the pursuit of disarmament as policy priorities over deterrence.

In contrast, Realists generally are skeptical of the prospects for the timely transformation of the "self-help" international system needed for disarmament. For many Realists, some states will likely acquire or sustain nuclear weapons as long as they are perceived as having security value in a dangerous international threat environment. Referring to the United States and Soviet Union during the Cold War, Kenneth Waltz observed that, "Their instincts for self-preservation call forth such efforts,"[124] and concluded that: "It is far more sensible to face the fact that nuclear weapons are here to stay...We should ask how we can continue to reap the benefits of nuclear weapons while reducing the dangers inherent in them."[125]

Thus, Realists tend to prioritize sustaining nuclear deterrence capabilities because in the context of an anarchic and nuclear-armed threat environment they may be needed to deter nuclear wars and wars that could escalate to nuclear employment. This conclusion is a logical consequence of Realist views of the anarchic structure of the international system, the associated enduring security dilemma, and the priority goal of national decision-making, i.e., national survival.

In short, for these Realists, the fear of national destruction in a nuclear war compels leaders in a nuclear balance of terror to "draw back from the brink" and enforces a cautious if grudging peace.[126] In contrast, Idealists seek via consensus a cooperative global order or centralized authority that establishes the benign conditions needed for peace and disarmament. These Realists and Idealists envisage very different motives and means to prevent nuclear war — fear leading to deterrence or to

---

[124] Kenneth Waltz, *Theory of International Politics* (Boston: McGraw Hill, 1979), p. 185.

[125] Waltz in, Sagan and Waltz, *The Spread of Nuclear Weapons: A Debate Renewed*, op. cit., p. 152.

[126] Ibid., p. 109.

cooperation leading to disarmament, respectively. Correspondingly, they call for very different national policy priorities, but their anticipated outcomes are the same.

Indeed, it is ironic that, as noted, some proponents of nuclear disarmament critique those Realists with optimistic expectations about deterrence as "nuclear romantics" because those expectations are based on the presumption of national leaders consistently behaving prudently and sensibly. However, the proposition that national leaders will consistently respond prudently and sensibly to the threat of nuclear weapons is no more key to confident expectations about deterrence than it is to the expectation that leaderships' prudent and sensible actions will enable international cooperation, global transformation and disarmament. Both narratives posit consistently prudent and sensible national responses to nuclear weapons. Neither addresses the committed martyr. If this is unrealistic and reflects nuclear romanticism on the part of those who have great confidence in deterrence, it would seem to reflect the same of those who contend that national leaders will achieve the international consensus and cooperation needed for benign global transformation and disarmament. Both deterrence optimism and the contemporary disarmament agenda are predicated on the expectation of consistently prudent and sensible actions of national leaders.

The Cold War ended peacefully with the collapse of the Soviet Union and its Warsaw Pact alliance. However, in a seeming confirmation of the Realist description of anarchic international relations and the power of mistrust to shape behavior, neither Russia nor China embraced the Western post-Cold War nuclear disarmament campaign.

The dilemma that now confronts us is that both Idealism and Realism appear to have captured truths about *what should be and what is*, respectively. The Idealist's contemporary focus on the humanitarian consequences of nuclear war surely is valid: *the risks to humanity of the employment of nuclear weapons are simply so extreme in so many scenarios that nuclear war must be prevented.* But, the contention that nuclear disarmament is the answer and, correspondingly, that nuclear deterrence must be demoted presumes that the necessary cooperative transformation of the interstate system is likely within a meaningful time frame.

Yet, downgrading nuclear deterrence now in favor of transformation and disarmament risks "waiting for Godot" because also valid is the Realist's basic contention that *the timely transformation of the interstate system needed for cooperative global nuclear disarmament appears implausible in the extreme.* Why? Because as John Mearsheimer concludes with understatement, "It is unlikely that all the great powers will simultaneously undergo an epiphany...,"[127] and, "there is little reason to think that change is in the offing."[128]   There are powerful and seemingly enduring structural factors working against benign transformation, as is illustrated by millennia of historical experience. *Leaderships around the world clearly are willing to take risks to expand or protect their national position, power and sovereignty. But, will they do so consciously, intentionally and repeatedly in ways that diminish their national sovereignty and power, and would very likely threaten their security if opponents are not similarly and reliably enlightened?* It certainly seems that the burden of proof is on those Idealists who posit an unprecedented and profound transformation of the international order to be forthcoming.   The apparent tranquility of the immediate post-Cold War period that led many to some optimism in this regard no longer exists.

The two truths that nuclear war *must be prevented* and that the global transformation needed for disarmament

---

[127] John Mearsheimer, "Realists as Idealists," *Security Studies*, Vol. 20, No. 3 (2011), p. 428.

[128] Mearsheimer, *The Tragedy of Great Power Politics*, p. 362.

perpetually appears to be nowhere in sight mean that — at least for the contemporary period of resurgent nuclear threats to the West — a dowdy Realist conclusion holds: deterrence combined with diplomacy must be given priority as the least miserable option now available to prevent nuclear war. This conclusion should not be controversial. In 2016, Secretary of Defense for the Obama Administration, Ashton Carter, emphasized publicly that "America's nuclear deterrence is the bedrock of our security and the Defense Department's highest priority mission." He added that, "We all, of course, would wish to live in a world without nuclear weapons...unfortunately, given what we see in today's security environment, it's also likely that our children and their children will probably have to live in a world where nuclear weapons exist."[129] More recently, the

---

[129] See Secretary of Defense Ashton Carter, "Remarks by Secretary Carter to Troops at Minot Air Force Base, North Dakota," September 26, 2016, available at https://www.defense.gov/Newsroom/Transcripts/Transcript/Article /956079/remarks-by-secretary-carter-to-troops-at-minot-air-force-base-north-dakota/. The bipartisan Perry-Schlesinger Commission concluded in its 2009 final report: "The United States must retain nuclear weapons until such time as the international environment may permit their elimination globally." See, Congressional Strategic Posture Commission, *America's Strategic Posture*, p. 17. In 1997, Clinton Administration Under Secretary of Defense for Policy, Walter Slocombe, concluded presciently that: "some argued, even in the Cold War, that the risk of possessing [nuclear] weapons far outweighed their benefits. I do not agree. Nuclear deterrence helped buy us time for internal forces of upheaval and decay to rend the Soviet Union and the Warsaw Pact and bring an end to the Cold War... We cannot be so certain of future Russian politics as to ignore the possibility that we would need again to deter the Russian nuclear force... In view of this, it would be irresponsible to dismantle the well-established — and much reduced — system of deterrence before new and reliable systems for preserving stability are in place." See, Senate Governmental Affairs Committee, Subcommittee on International Security, Proliferation and Federal Services, *Statement of the Honorable Walter B. Slocombe, Undersecretary of Defense for Policy, Hearing on Nuclear Weapons and Deterrence*, February 12, 1997, pp. 3, 5. The basic conclusion that nuclear deterrence should be

Obama Administration's Assistant Secretary of State for Arms Control, Frank Rose, observed similarly: "In the last 25 years, we've been too focused on reducing the numbers of weapons and not on enhancing a stable deterrence with the objective of preventing miscalculations. My No. 1 priority is preventing nuclear use. And if we don't reduce a single additional nuclear weapon, but we don't have a nuclear detonation, that's success."[130]

While it may seem counterintuitive, the goal of precluding nuclear conflict to the extent possible does not necessarily point to the wisdom of placing policy priority on nuclear disarmament now. It is not the path when, in an enduringly anarchic international system, U.S. disarmament moves could degrade the functioning of deterrence and thereby increase the risk of war. Every prudent step must be made to ensure that deterrence is as secure, credible, reliable and safe as possible. Doing so certainly is compatible with complementary diplomacy.

These conclusions—that sustaining credible nuclear deterrence is likely a safer alternative than devaluing it in serious expectation of timely international transformation and nuclear disarmament—admittedly reflect speculation about alternative futures that is based on the manifest resilience of the international system's anarchic structure and inference from history and patterns of leadership behavior.[131] Simply stated, in the current international threat environment there would seem to be greater

---

accepted and sustained as an interim measure until an alternative global order enables disarmament was reached by the U.S. Conference of Catholic Bishops in 1983. See, "The Challenge of Peace: God's Promise and Our Response," op. cit., p. 18.

[130] Quoted in, Kenji Minemura, "Obama Arms Official: Nuclear Deterrence Must be Strengthened," *Asahi Shimbun Online*, September 10, 2019, available at http://www.asahi.com/ajw/articles/AJ201909100011.html.

[131] Waltz, "The Spread of Nuclear Weapons: More May be Better," op. cit.

potential risk in the prioritization of nuclear disarmament by Western powers in the expectation of a new, cooperative world order than in the Western preservation of nuclear deterrence. Such speculation is resistant to serious probabilistic prediction. However, given mounting contemporary threats to the West, including nuclear, the premature degrading of nuclear deterrence could indeed unintentionally precipitate its failure — as 1930s disarmament efforts clearly contributed to the road to World War II.[132] Others obviously disagree with these conclusions — hence the potential value of a worthy debate vice dueling monologues.

With the Cold War long over, and the subsequent great optimism about a "New World Order" long gone, it remains to be seen whether Realists and Idealists will now begin to engage each other on nuclear policy issues at the level of ideas and with a degree of mutual respect and decorum, or will continue to engage largely within their own respective closed circles and echo chambers. The path of least resistance favors the latter. If so, the character and content of the U.S. nuclear "debate" will almost certainly remain a matter of competing voices repetitively talking past one another.

In contrast, those participating in the market place of ideas regarding nuclear disarmament could, without acrimony, identify and defend to the extent possible the Realist and Idealist philosophic foundations of their competing positions. For example, Realists might explain why we should limit our expectations regarding future leadership decision-making and states' behavior to established patterns, past and present. Why is the prospect for timely, profound cooperative change of the international system so remote as to be implausible? There are some past

---

[132] See Brad Roberts, "Nuclear Ethics and the Ban Treaty," in *Nuclear Disarmament*, Bård Nikolas, Vik Steen and Olav Njølstad, eds. (London: Routledge, 2019), p. 124.

examples of profound changes in the structure of human relations, such as the creation of the nation-state system itself. Why then is the systemic transformation envisaged by Idealists *implausible*?

Idealists in turn might explain why, *at this point in history*, we should seriously expect diverse national leaderships to achieve the enlightened interstate trust, consensus, and cooperation needed to transform the international order and disarm—beyond the unconvincing assertions that it can happen because it must, or because "no law of nature stands in the way." No law of nature precludes the cooperative resolution of conflicting interests *within* individual state borders wherein some form of central authority exists. But it would seem imprudent for government officials to plan as if horrific domestic criminal violence—which claims approximately 500,000 lives every year globally—will end anytime soon by the application of reason and enlightened self-interest.

An engagement so emphasizing the transparency of the different philosophic origins underlying contending Idealist and Realist positions on disarmament and deterrence would likely demand an unprecedented level of introspection on the part of many participants. The competing positions could well remain irreconcilable. Nevertheless, greater transparency with regard to the philosophical origins and logic of these dueling positions and their most significant points of departure would add substance to the superficial language and callings that often dominate public discourse. This would help provide listening leaders and policy makers the privilege of making more informed comparisons of the veracity of these competing positions—and at least the potential for more edified nuclear policy discussions.

Chapter 2
Is Deterrence Easy or Difficult?
The Great Divide in U.S.
Deterrence Thought

"In spite of our reliance on the idea that deterrence will work, we usually do not analyze carefully the basic concepts behind such a policy. This somewhat lackadaisical interest in bedrock concepts is probably related to a subconscious fear that our foundations cannot stand close examination."

Herman Kahn, 1959

Introduction

The previous chapter describes contrary Realist and Idealist views regarding the feasibility of a timely and cooperative transformation of the international order needed for nuclear disarmament. Their differing expectations often drive conflicting narratives regarding nuclear disarmament. These different Realist and Idealist expectations help to explain much of the U.S. policy debate on the matter. However, they do not help much to explain the decades-long U.S. interrelated debates about nuclear deterrence and the value of physical defenses against nuclear attack.

Also as noted in Chapter 1, U.S. nuclear policy has been dominated by Realist thought. The deep differences in the U.S. policy debate regarding deterrence strategies and the value of physical defenses often reflect divisions *among Realists* on the subjects, *not* the familiar divide separating Realists and Idealists. The U.S. deterrence policy debate is largely a reflection of two competing deterrence narratives that share some initial Realist roots, but then diverge in significant ways. These are referred to here as the "easy" and "difficult" deterrence narratives. They posit very different expectations about leadership decision-making and how deterrence is likely to function, leading to conflicting positions regarding deterrence requirements and the conditions needed for "stability." Unsurprisingly perhaps, these two conflicting narratives point to the evidence of history to support their particular positions on deterrence and its requirements.

Both the easy and difficult deterrence narratives concur that nuclear deterrence is valuable, even necessary for now, given a general skepticism about the prospects for the timely transformation of the international system and disarmament. "Nuclear weapons are here to stay...We should ask how we can continue to reap the deterrence benefits of nuclear weapons while reducing the dangers inherent in them."[1] However, while sharing some initial Realist assumptions, the easy and difficult deterrence narratives differ on the question of how best to deter. They differ sharply on the ease or challenge of acquiring and maintaining effective deterrence capabilities. With few exceptions, this has been the question at the heart of the U.S. nuclear debate for seven decades—not whether the United States should demote nuclear deterrence and, correspondingly, place policy priority on the pursuit of global disarmament.

There are additional contemporary issues of interest regarding deterrence, including the implications of cross-domain and cyber threats. But the return of great power competition and frequent explicit nuclear threats to the United States and allies has rightly highlighted the need for

---

[1] Kenneth Waltz in, Scott Sagan and Kenneth N. Waltz, *The Spread of Nuclear Weapons: A Debate Renewed* (New York: Norton and Co., 2003), p.152.

a renewed understanding of nuclear deterrence following an almost two-decade hiatus.[2]

The "Easy" Deterrence Narrative

During the Cold War, renowned academics, including Kenneth Waltz, Thomas Schelling, Bernard Brodie, and Robert Jervis advanced basic points of an enduring narrative about mutual nuclear deterrence commonly referred to as a "stable balance of terror" — "stable" meaning that neither side would have irresistible incentives to employ nuclear weapons or engage in provocations that would likely escalate to nuclear use. The simplified (and popularized) easy deterrence narrative is a pastiche or patchwork conceptual construct that draws from these scholars' innovative analyses. It incorporates various points appearing in their works, but does not reliably reflect the variation, subtlety or nuance of their works. The discussion here *does not suggest* that Waltz, Schelling, Brodie or Jervis necessarily advanced or even accepted all facets of the easy deterrence narrative—but that it incorporates various select points found in their works.

This deterrence narrative posits that the essential requirements for stable mutual deterrence are easy to understand and meet and, correspondingly, that the functioning of mutual deterrence should be considered largely predictable and reliable. Those deterrence requirements are: rational, "sensible" leadership decision-making (or possibly less demanding "common sense"),[3] and properly controlled and safeguarded capabilities for

---

[2] See for example, Curtis McGiffin, "The Lost Art of Deterrence Education," *Information Series*, National Institute for Public Policy, No. 446 (October 2, 2019), p. 2.

[3] Waltz contends that rational calculations are *not* necessary for nuclear deterrence to function, "only a little common sense." Sagan and Waltz, op. cit., p.154.

strategic nuclear retaliation even after suffering an attack, i.e., a "survivable second-strike capability."   Schelling concluded that with such second-strike capabilities, "a powerfully stable mutual deterrence results."[4]

The "second-strike" strategic nuclear capability needed for this stable nuclear "balance of terror" is easily acquired and maintained: "It does not take much to deter...in the nuclear business deterrence is cheap and easy;"[5] "the invulnerability of a sufficient number of warheads is easy to achieve...With nuclear weapons, [deterrence] stability and peace rest on easy calculation of what one country can do to another;"[6] and, "The healthy fear of devastation, which cannot be exorcised short of the attainment of a first-strike capability, makes deterrence relatively easy."[7]   This narrative of relatively easy deterrence survived the Cold War and continues to be a powerful theme in public discussions of deterrence and its requirements.

Some scholars suggest that such high confidence in the "easy" and reliable efficacy of mutual nuclear deterrence is "a utopian and ahistorical kind of thinking totally contrary to traditional Realist philosophy."[8]   There is a reasonable

---

[4] Thomas Schelling, *The Strategy of Conflict* (Cambridge, Mass.: Harvard University Press, 1960), p. 251.

[5] Waltz in, Sagan and Waltz, op. cit., pp. 142, 152.

[6] Kenneth N. Waltz, "Nuclear Myths and Political Realities," *The American Political Science Review*, Vol. 84, No. 3 (September 1990), pp. 732, 734.

[7] Robert Jervis, "Why Nuclear Superiority Doesn't Matter," *Political Science Quarterly*, Vol. 94, No. 4 (Winter 1979-1980), pp. 617-618.

[8] Campbell Craig, *Glimmer of a New Leviathan: Total War in the Realism of Niebuhr, Morgenthau, and Waltz* (NY: Columbia University Press, 2007), p. 172. Richard Betts uses the term "utopian realists" to describe the confidence in nuclear deterrence evidenced by Waltz and other Realists. See Richard K. Betts, "Universal Deterrence or Conceptual Collapse? Liberal Pessimism and Utopian Realism," in, *The Coming Crisis: Nuclear Proliferation, U.S. Interests, and World Order*, Victor A. Utgoff, ed. (Cambridge, Mass: MIT Press, 2000), p. 52.

argument behind this point. However, the confidence of the easy deterrence narrative follows in part from three traditional Realist tenets: the international system is anarchic with mistrust among its members; in this system great powers generally prioritize the pursuit of national survival in their decision-making, and do so rationally.[9] Easy deterrence confidence follows from both a macro view of the international system and its anarchic structure and from the expectation that individual units, i.e., countries, will behave in predictable ways when facing a severe nuclear threat. Leaderships able to reason will seek to avoid those actions that could precipitate an opponent's devastating nuclear attack. As Waltz states, "Deterrent policies derive from structural theory, which emphasizes that the units of an international political system must tend to their own security as best they can.... A little reasoning leads to the conclusions that to fight nuclear wars is impossible and that to launch an offensive that might prompt nuclear retaliation is obvious folly. To reach those conclusions, complicated calculations are not required...[Deterrence] depends on fear. To create fear, nuclear weapons are the best possible means;"[10] and, "In a nuclear world, to act in blatantly offensive ways is madness."[11] In short, this deterrence narrative tends to assume that the priority goal of protecting national survival and the fear naturally created by nuclear weapons combine to compel caution and provide easy deterrence.

---

[9] These are Realist "bedrock assumptions." See, John J. Mearsheimer, *The Tragedy of Great Power Politics* (New York: W.W. Norton & Co., 2001), pp. 30-31.

[10] Waltz in, Sagan and Waltz, op. cit., p. 154.

[11] Kenneth Waltz, "The Spread of Nuclear Weapons: More May be Better," *Adelphi Papers*, Number 171 (London: International Institute for Strategic Studies, 1981), available at https://www.mtholyoke.edu/acad/intrel/waltz1.htm.

In 1983, a Harvard Nuclear Study Group observed that since the establishment of nuclear deterrence, the international system had avoided great power war despite many pressures that previously would likely have triggered conflict. The Study Group attributed this stability to the nuclear "balance of terror." Why this unprecedented stability? Because, "Nuclear weapons have created what we call the *crystal ball effect*...This crystal ball effect helps to give the nuclear world at least some measure of stability. Statesmen in the atomic age can envision the destruction of a full-scale nuclear war and it makes them determined to avoid it."[12]

Using the same "crystal ball" metaphor, Waltz points to the *unique* effectiveness of nuclear weapons for deterrence: "With conventional weapons, the crystal ball is clouded. With nuclear weapons, it is perfectly clear;"[13] "The catastrophe promised by nuclear war contrasts sharply with the extreme difficulty of predicting outcomes among conventional competitors;"[14] and, "In a conventional world, deterrent threats are ineffective because the damage threatened is distant, limited, and problematic. Nuclear weapons make military miscalculations difficult and politically pertinent prediction easy."[15]

The same national security priority and caution that compel leaders in an anarchic system to be wary of Idealist proposals for global transformation and nuclear disarmament also compel them to avoid nuclear war or conflict that could escalate to nuclear war. The threat of

---

[12] Albert Carnesale, et al., *Living with Nuclear Weapons* (New York: Bantam Books, 1983), p. 44. See also, Gordon Craig and Alexander George, *Force and Statecraft: Diplomatic Problems of Our Time* (New York: Oxford University Press, 1995), p. 225.

[13] Waltz in, Sagan and Waltz, op. cit., p. 114.

[14] Waltz, "Nuclear Myths and Political Realities," op. cit., p. 734.

[15] Waltz, "The Spread of Nuclear Weapons: More May be Better," op. cit.

nuclear weapons poses a problem and also presents a potential solution to the problem: A properly structured balance of terror is an overwhelmingly powerful deterrent because leaders must be cautious when national survival is at risk. This is the apparent meaning of Waltz's central point regarding deterrence: "In applying theories, one considers salient conditions in the world, and nothing is more salient than nuclear weapons."[16]

President John Kennedy's National Security Advisor McGeorge Bundy observed that U.S. and Soviet Cold War decision-making reflected this powerful peacekeeping effect of nuclear deterrence: "The stalemate that keeps nuclear peace between the superpowers is so deep and strong that it is not affected by the relative ruthlessness of the two societies or their different experience of twentieth-century war. What each can do to the other, whoever goes first, is more than enough to stay every hand that does not belong to a madman... The imperative of avoiding nuclear war imposes great caution on both governments."[17]

Bundy expected that this powerful deterrent effect would apply to leaders who are not "madmen" because the fear of nuclear destruction overcomes any reasoning leadership's particular goals and characteristics, or a country's history or culture. Waltz elaborated on the same expectation: "Differences among nuclear countries abound, but for keeping the peace what difference have they made?...In a nuclear world, any state—whether ruled by Stalin, a Mao Zedong, a Saddam Hussein, or a Kim Jong Il—will be deterred by the knowledge that aggressive actions may lead to its own destruction....Who cares about the [differing] 'cognitive' abilities of leaders when nobody but an idiot can fail to comprehend [nuclear weapons']

---

[16] Waltz in, Sagan and Waltz, op. cit., p. 154.

[17] McGeorge Bundy, *Danger and Survival: Choices About the Bomb in the First Fifty Years* (New York: Random House, 1988), p. 592.

destructive force." [18] And, "In a nuclear world any state will be deterred by another state's second-strike forces. One need not become preoccupied with characteristics of the state that is to be deterred or scrutinize its leaders."[19]

Why so? Because, as Bundy elaborated, "In the real world of real political leaders—whether here or in the Soviet Union—a decision that would bring even one hydrogen bomb on one city of one's own country would be recognized in advance as a catastrophic blunder; ten bombs on ten cities would be a disaster beyond history; and a hundred bombs on a hundred cities are unthinkable."[20]

For leaders who are not "mad," war between nuclear powers in a proper balance of terror simply *must* be avoided—no goal short of national survival could justify an action that would seriously risk "unthinkable" national destruction. Thus, "if decisionmakers are 'sensible,' peace is the most likely outcome."[21] This expectation regarding leadership decision-making inspires confidence in the predictable functioning of nuclear deterrence among states. Indeed, Bundy coined the term "existential deterrence" — meaning that a balance of terror creates the conditions needed for effective mutual deterrence without regard to many other factors—including the character of the sides involved or their relative nuclear capabilities: "The terrible

---

[18] Waltz in, Sagan and Waltz, op. cit., pp. 117, 132.

[19] Waltz, "Nuclear Myths and Political Realities," op. cit., pp. 737-738. Almost two decades later, George Washington University professor James Lebovic, repeats Waltz's point and asserts that: "In actuality, it matters little whether US enemies are barbarously hateful and vengeful, or ruthlessly insensitive to cost." See *Deterring International Terrorism and Rogue States* (New York: Routledge, 2007), p. 29. See also James Wood Forsyth Jr., "Nuclear Weapons and Political Behavior," *Strategic Studies Quarterly*, Vol. 11, No. 3 (Fall 2017), pp. 116, 120.

[20] McGeorge Bundy, "To Cap the Volcano," *Foreign Affairs*, Vol. 48, No. 1 (October 1969), p. 10.

[21] Robert Jervis, "The Political Effects of Nuclear Weapons: A Comment," *International Security*, Vol. 13, No. 2 (Fall 1988), p. 81.

and unavoidable uncertainties in any recourse to nuclear war create what could be called 'existential' deterrence, where the function of the adjective is to distinguish this phenomenon from anything based on strategic theories or declared policies...As long as each side has thermonuclear weapons that could be used against the opponent, even after the strongest possible preemptive attack [a "second-strike capability"], existential deterrence is strong..."[22] Waltz concurred: "The [deterrence] effects of nuclear weapons derive not from any particular design for their employment in war but simply from their presence."[23]

The easy deterrence narrative attributes considerable confidence in a balance of nuclear terror to produce the reliable functioning of mutual deterrence, and U.S. policy statements have often reflected this confidence. There are numerous popular, expert, and official Cold War and post-Cold War illustrations of this confidence in the predictable effect of nuclear deterrence. Several will suffice to demonstrate the point:

> In U.S.-Soviet relations, the current nuclear postures have substantially solved the problem of deterring deliberate nuclear attack. Under present conditions, no rational leader could conclude that his or her nation would be better off with a nuclear war than without one.[24]

---

[22] McGeorge Bundy, "Bishops and the Bomb," *New York Review of Books*, Vol. 30, No. 10 (June 16, 1983), pp. 3-4. See also, Bernard Brodie, *War and Politics* (New York: Macmillan Publishing, 1973), p. 412.

[23] Waltz, "Nuclear Myths and Political Realities," op. cit., p. 738.

[24] Graham Allison, Albert Carnesale, and Joseph Nye, "Conclusion," in, *Fateful Visions: Avoiding Nuclear Catastrophe*, Joseph Nye, Graham Allison, and Albert Carnesale, eds. (Cambridge, Mass: Ballinger Publishing, 1988), p. 216.

The probability of major war among states having nuclear weapons approaches zero.[25]

Deterrence *is ensured* by having a survivable [nuclear] capability to hold at risk what potentially hostile leaders value, and we will maintain that capability.[26]

In the light of the certain prospect of retaliation there has been literally no chance at all that any sane political authority, in either the United States or the Soviet Union, would consciously choose to start a nuclear war. This proposition is true for the past, the present, and the foreseeable future. For sane men on both sides, the balance of terror is overwhelmingly persuasive.[27]

Unless we are dealing with utter madmen, there is no conceivable reason why in any necessary showdown with the Soviet Union, appropriate manipulations of force and threats of force, certainly coordinated with more positive diplomatic maneuvers, cannot bring about deterrence. That is one respect in which the world is utterly different now from what it was in 1939 or 1914, when deterrence, however effective temporarily, had the final intrinsic weakness that one side or both did not truly fear what we would now call general war.[28]

Our conclusion, in its narrowest terms, must be that the deliberate resort to war by a nuclear power

---

[25] Waltz, "Nuclear Myths and Political Realities," op. cit., p. 740.

[26] John Deutch, Testimony in, U.S. House, Committee on Foreign Affairs, *U.S. Nuclear Policy: Hearings*, 103rd Congress, 2nd Session (Washington, D.C.: USGPO, 1995), p. 36. (Emphasis added).

[27] Bundy, "To Cap the Volcano," *Foreign Affairs*, op. cit., p. 9.

[28] Bernard Brodie, *Escalation and the Nuclear Option* (Princeton, NJ: Princeton University Press, 1966), p. 74.

against a power capable of effective retaliation is permanently ruled out...the deliberate resort to major nonnuclear warfare between such powers is also ruled out. And the resort to even such limited warfare as border skirmishes between them is notably inhibited by the danger that it would escalate out of control, ending in nuclear war.[29]

Nuclear deterrence worked throughout the Cold War, it continues to work now, it will work into the future...The exact same kinds of nuclear deterrence calculations that have always worked will continue to work.[30]

What deters them today is what will always deter them—the certainty that if they attack us with weapons of mass destruction their regimes will be destroyed. In other words, what is protecting us right now from the most likely rogue threat...is classic deterrence.[31]

No regime, no matter how aggressive and risk-inclined, would be so foolish as to attack the United States, a move that would yield little advantage, and thereby incur an attack's clear consequence—utter destruction.[32]

---

[29] Louis Halle, "Does War Have a Future?" *Foreign Affairs*, Vol. 52, No. 1 (October 1973), p. 23.

[30] Principal Deputy Undersecretary of Defense Jan Lodal in, Jan Lodal (P)DUSD and Ashton Carter ASD (International Security), with selected reporters, 31 July 1995, Washington, D.C., News Conference Transcript, 9-10 (mimeographed).

[31] Thomas Friedman, "Who's Crazy Here," *The New York Times*, June 25, 2001, p. 25.

[32] Elbridge Colby, "Restoring Deterrence," *Orbis*, Vol. 51, No. 3 (Summer 2007), p. 419.

In short, this narrative deems nuclear deterrence to be reliably effective in preventing large-scale attacks. This sanguine perspective may be surprising given the dark outlook typically attributed to Realism. Nevertheless, in the absence of "madmen," the "crystal ball" effect unique to nuclear weapons is expected to provide even the most aggressive leadership with clarity regarding the intolerable catastrophe that would attend nuclear conflict, thus "ensuring" the deterrence of nuclear war and conflicts considered likely to escalate to nuclear war.

Whereas the contemporary Idealist disarmament narrative identifies the fear of nuclear weapons as the catalyst for the global transformation needed to enable disarmament, this deterrence narrative envisages the fear of nuclear weapons as reliably minimizing the prospects for nuclear war or large-scale attack. For Idealists, the potential use of nuclear weapons is the existential problem and demoting nuclear deterrence in pursuit of international transformation and disarmament is the solution. For those who are sanguine about the easy and reliable functioning of deterrence, the potential for war is the problem but the deterrent effects available via a nuclear balance of terror prevent it.

Easy Deterrence: How Much Is Enough?

As noted, traditional Realist assumptions contribute to an expectation of the relatively predictable and effective functioning of nuclear deterrence. Several elaborations on these assumptions, however, lead to the conclusion of deterrence ease and relatively modest requirements. These added elaborations are *not* integral to traditional Realist thought per se; they are "extra-Realist" expectations about leadership decision-making and the functioning of deterrence.

Societal Threats

First, this narrative of easy and reliable deterrence typically contends that the nuclear "second-strike" capabilities needed for deterrence *are the survivable forces required to threaten punishment on an opponent's societal assets.* Nuclear capability *beyond* that needed to threaten societal destruction does not add to deterrence; it is unnecessary "overkill."[33] The expectation that a punitive threat of societal destruction can serve as the basic measure of adequacy for reliable deterrence was particularly prominent in Cold War academic treatments of the subject and also in many official U.S. declarations regarding deterrence. Societal assets could include cities, industry, power, transportation, population, etc., but from early in the Cold War, threats to population and cities became a type of shorthand for measuring deterrence strategies based on threats to an opponent's societal assets: "A force sufficient to kill the enemy's population and destroy his wealth is an adequate deterrent,"[34] and, "Deterrence comes from having enough to destroy the other's cities; this capability is an absolute, not a relative, one."[35] The expectation of effective

---

[33] See for example, Herbert York, *Race to Oblivion* (New York: Simon and Schuster, 1970), pp. 42, 46-48.

[34] Ralph Lapp, *Kill and Overkill: The Strategy of Annihilation* (New York: Basic Books, 1962), p. 140.

[35] Jervis, "Why Nuclear Superiority Doesn't Matter," op. cit., p. 618. And, "We should find virtue in the technological discoveries that enhance the anti-population potency of our retaliatory weapons." Schelling, op. cit., p. 239, see also pp. 233 and 236-237; and Thomas Schelling, "Reciprocal Measures for Arms Stabilization," in, *Arms Control, Disarmament, And National Security*, Donald Brennan, ed. (New York: George Braziller, 1961), p. 167. See also, York, op. cit., pp. 42, 46-48; McGeorge Bundy, William J. Crowe, Jr., and Sidney D. Drell, *Reducing Nuclear Danger* (New York: Council on Foreign Relations Press, 1993), p. 95; Bernard Brodie, "The Anatomy of Deterrence," *World Politics*, Vol. 11, No. 2 (January 1959), p. 177; and Jerome H. Kahan,

deterrence from societal threats ("cities") has continued to be a theme in public commentary in the post-Cold War era: "Deterrence today would remain stable even if retaliation against only ten cities were assured."[36]

This general expectation that punitive threats against an opponent's society will deter reliably is *not* based on the unreasonable presumption that all opponents are enlightened and dutiful civil servants. Instead: "What government would risk sudden losses of such proportion or indeed of much lesser proportion? Rulers want to have a country that they can continue to rule," [37] and this would be put at risk by nuclear deterrent threats to their societies.

This focus on deterrence strategies based on threatening an opponent's society provides much of the basis for the narrative's contention that deterrence is "easy" because threatening an opponent's societal targets establishes a relatively low standard of adequacy for U.S. nuclear force numbers. Great societal assets generally are relatively few, undefended, and highly vulnerable to modest numbers of nuclear weapons.[38]   Deterrence works reliably and predictably at nuclear force levels that are easy to acquire and maintain because opponents with a modicum of "common sense" will place decisive value on the preservation of their nation's societal assets. Thus, they can be deterred from highly provocative actions by modestly defined second-strike capabilities.

Security in the Nuclear Age (Washington, D.C.: The Brookings Institution, 1975), p. 330.

[36] Bruce Blair, et al., "Smaller and Safer," *Foreign Affairs*, Vol. 89, No. 5 (September-October 2010), p. 10.

[37] Waltz, "The Spread of Nuclear Weapons: More May be Better," op. cit.

[38] As noted in, Steven Pifer and Michael E. O'Hanlon, *The Opportunity: Next Steps in Reducing Nuclear Arms* (Washington, D.C.: Brookings Institution Press, 2012), pp. 20-21.

Confidence in deterrence based on societal threats was not limited to academic discussions. In the 1960s, Secretary of Defense Robert McNamara's *public and then-classified pronouncements* regarding nuclear deterrence specified the U.S. threat levels to Soviet society (population and industry) considered adequate for reliable nuclear deterrence. The precise numbers of his "assured destruction" requirement for U.S. deterrence capabilities shifted somewhat over time, but in the now declassified 1964 *Draft Presidential Memorandum*, Secretary McNamara defined U.S. deterrence requirements as the U.S. ability to destroy "25 percent of [Soviet] population (55 million people) and more than two-thirds of [Soviet] industrial capacity."[39]   Secretary McNamara expressed confidence in the effectiveness of this nuclear deterrence threat: "Such a capability would, with a high degree of confidence, ensure that we could deter under all foreseeable conditions, a calculated, deliberate nuclear attack on the United States."[40]   In short, by the mid-1960s, Secretary McNamara expressed great confidence in the reliability of this type of deterrence threat. He "had come to believe that the U.S. deterrent capability, the nation's strategic offensive forces, not the damage-limiting strategic defensive forces, protected American society."[41]

There was nothing magical about Secretary McNamara's "assured destruction" metric for deterrence. It represented the "flat of the curve" with regard to the number of U.S. nuclear weapons needed to threaten the

---

[39]*Draft Memorandum for the President, Secretary of Defense to the President [Lyndon B. Johnson], Subj: Recommended FY 1966-FY1970 Programs for Strategic Offensive Forces, Continental Air and Missile Defense Forces, and Civil Defense*, December 3, 1964, p. 4 (Sanitized and declassified on January 5, 1983). Hereafter, Secretary McNamara, *DPM, 1964*.

[40] Secretary McNamara, *DPM, 1964*, p. 4.

[41] Edward J. Drea, *Secretaries of Defense Historical Series, Vol. VI: McNamara, Clifford, and the Burdens of Vietnam, 1965-1969* (Washington, D.C.: Historical Office, Office of the Secretary of Defense, USGPO 2011), p. 347.

specified levels of destruction on the Soviet population and industry. Beyond a specific number of weapons, the additional level of societal destruction possible with each additional weapon rapidly diminished. The force level associated with that "flat of the curve" for additional weapons and consequent societal destruction became the defining level of societal destruction declared necessary for deterrence and thus the measure of forces declared adequate for deterrence. The computation of the declining marginal value of additional U.S. nuclear weapons against Soviet societal targets determined the percentiles declared as deterrence standards and the capabilities necessary to meet those standards.[42] Secretary McNamara's mid-1960s "worst-case" estimate of projected U.S. nuclear weapon requirements to meet his "assured destruction" standard numbered into the thousands,[43] and he emphasized that his deterrence metric did not reflect how the United States would actually employ nuclear weapons in the event of war.[44]

Nevertheless, a particular "theory of limitations" for deterrence requirements emerged from the expectation that all "sensible" leaders prioritize national survival and that *nuclear threats to an opponent's societal assets* would provide reliable deterrent effect. This deterrence narrative has since

---

[42] See Alain Enthoven and K. Wayne Smith, *How Much is Enough? Shaping the Defense Program, 1961-1969* (New York: Harper and Row, 1971), pp. 67, 207-208. And, Secretary McNamara, *DPM 1964*, op. cit., p. 17.

[43] Drea, op. cit., pp. 347, 353.

[44] *Draft Memorandum for the President, Secretary of Defense [Robert S. McNamara] to the President [Lyndon B. Johnson], Subj: Recommended FY 1965-FY 1969 Strategic Retaliatory Forces*, December 6, 1963, p. I-12. (Sanitized and declassified on January 5, 1983). See also, *Draft Memorandum for the President, Secretary of Defense [Robert S. McNamara] to the President [Lyndon B. Johnson], Subj: Strategic Offensive and Defensive Forces*, January 15, 1968, p. 9. (Sanitized and declassified on January 5, 1983).

become perhaps the single most prominent and enduring theme in public commentary about U.S. nuclear deterrence requirements. There is no single commonly agreed number of nuclear weapons deemed adequate for deterrence based on punitive threats to an opponent's societal assets. However, many commentaries suggest a range from "hundreds" to far fewer.[45] Again, a few examples across decades illustrate this point:

> The number of nuclear weapons required to deter policymakers in "the real world" has long been far fewer than several thousand or even several hundred. It may be much closer to the simplest number of all: one.[46]

> Would the Soviets be deterred by the prospect of losing ten cities? Or two cities? No one knows, although one might intuitively guess that the threshold is closer to ten than to either two or fifty.[47]

> Most professional analysts of the subject believe that the prospect of about one hundred thermonuclear warheads exploding over urban areas is more than enough to deter either side from starting a nuclear war...I personally believe that very much smaller numbers are sufficient to deter war; I have used numbers like one hundred only because it is customary to do so in such arguments, and because the above arguments do not hinge on whether the

---

[45] See a listing of such recommendations in, Keith B. Payne and James R. Schlesinger, *Minimum Deterrence: Examining the Evidence* (Fairfax, VA: National Institute Press, 2013), pp. 4-5.

[46] Thomas M. Nichols, *No Use: Nuclear Weapons and U.S. National Security* (Philadelphia: University of Pennsylvania Press, 2014), p. 85.

[47] Glenn Snyder, *Deterrence and Defense: Toward a Theory of National Security* (Princeton, NJ: Princeton University Press, 1961), p. 57.

number is in fact one hundred or something very much smaller.[48]

Warheads numbered in the hundreds can destroy the United States and the Soviet Union as viable societies no matter what defensive measures they take. Deterrence works because nuclear weapons enable one state to punish another state severely without first defeating it.[49]

No current or conceivable threat to the United States requires it to maintain more than a few hundred survivable nuclear weapons. The delivery of fewer than a hundred warheads could destroy the society and economy of any country, and tens of detonations could kill more people than have ever been killed in any previous war.[50]

No sane adversary would believe that any political or military advantage would be worth a significant risk of the destruction of his own society…Thus ten to one hundred survivable warheads should be more than enough to deter any rational leader from ordering an attack on the cities of the United States or its allies.[51]

---

[48] York, op. cit., pp. 167-168.

[49] Waltz, "The Spread of Nuclear Weapons: More May be Better," op. cit.

[50] Union of Concerned Scientists, *The Obama Administration's New Nuclear Policy: An Assessment of the "Nuclear Posture Review,"* (Washington, D.C.: Union of Concerned Scientists, April 8, 2010), available at http://www.ucusa.org/nuclear_weapons_and_global_ security/nuclear_weapons/policy_issues/Obama-administration-npr.html.

[51] Steve Fetter, "Nuclear Strategy and Targeting Doctrine," in Harold A. Feiveson, ed., *The Nuclear Turning Point* (Washington, D.C.: Brookings Institution Press, 1999), p. 57.

Rather fewer than 100 warheads is sufficient to inflict a wholly unacceptable level of damage on a continental-sized economy, and suggest that — even for the most enthusiastic proponent of nuclear deterrence — maintaining an arsenal at a higher than that level is unnecessary.[52]

...a reasonably small force of several hundred weapons would allow that state to strike back over 100 times before it had to negotiate. No state on the planet could withstand that sort of punishment, and no sane leader would run that sort of risk.[53]

In short, this deterrence narrative paints a particular picture. It contends that deterrence is easy to achieve and sustain because a punitive nuclear threat of societal destruction will deter, requires relatively few weapons, and is made transparent by the "crystal ball effect." This expectation may reflect a degree of "mirror imaging," i.e., expecting U.S. leaders and opponents ultimately to perceive, calculate and behave in a similar, *and thus predictable* manner.[54] A modest survivable second-strike

---

[52] Gareth Evans and Yoriko Kawaguchi, *Eliminating Nuclear Threats: A Practical Agenda for Global Policymakers*, Report of the International Commission on Nuclear Non-proliferation and Disarmament (Canberra: International Commission on Nuclear Non-proliferation and Disarmament, 2009), p. 194.

[53] Forsyth, op. cit., p. 122.

[54] The Defense Department's Historical Office says of Secretary McNamara, "his mechanistic worldview assumed the [deterrence] logic of assured destruction motivated both Washington and Moscow to react in predictable ways." Drea, op. cit., p. 370. Thomas Schelling observed in this regard: "You can sit in your armchair and try to predict how people will behave by asking how you would behave if you had your wits about you. You get, free of charge, a lot of vicarious empirical behavior. Quoted in, Kathleen Archibald et al., *Strategic Interaction and Conflict: Original Papers and Discussion* (Berkeley, CA: Institute of International Studies, University of California, 1966), p. 150. Herbert York observed: "We imagine them trying to deter us as we try to deter

capability will serve to compel all but "mad" leaders to "draw back from the brink."[55] This indeed is a sanguine narrative.

Graduated Options for Deterrence

An important additional element of this easy deterrence narrative is the contention that U.S. capabilities for limited or "graduated" nuclear threats can help to deter limited attacks and prevent escalation in the event an initial failure of deterrence leads to limited conflict. Schelling, Waltz, and Jervis essentially endorsed the threat of "graduated" (limited) response options as part of a U.S. deterrence strategy to demonstrate U.S. will and thereby deter limited attacks and help control escalation if deterrence initially fails.[56] They identified the capability for graduated demonstration-of-will threats as particularly important for extending U.S. nuclear deterrence coverage to allies.

This rationale for graduated nuclear options is *not* based on the potential military effects of limited nuclear employment. It is based on the expectation that: 1) brandishing limited nuclear threats can help deter limited nuclear provocations by having proportional response options; and, 2) graduated threat options can help deter

---

them." See York's testimony in, U.S. Senate, Committee on Foreign Relations, Subcommittee on Arms Control, *ABM, MIRV, SALT, and the Nuclear Arms Race*, Hearings, 91st Congress, 2nd Session (Washington, D.C.: USGPO, 1970), p. 64.

55 Waltz in, Sagan and Waltz, op. cit., p. 109.

56 Thomas Schelling, *Arms and Influence* (New Haven, CT: Yale University Press, 1966), pp. 102-112; Thomas Schelling, "Comment," in *Limited Strategic War*, Klaus Knorr and Thornton Read, eds. (New York: Frederick Praeger Press, 1962), pp. 248-250; Thomas Schelling, "Surprise Attack and Disarmament," in *NATO and American Security*, Klaus Knorr, ed. (Princeton, NJ: Princeton University Press, 1959), p. 207; Waltz, "Nuclear Myths and Political Realities," op. cit., pp. 733-734; Jervis, "Why Nuclear Superiority Doesn't Matter," op. cit., pp. 618, 628-629.

escalation if deterrence initially fails by demonstrating U.S. resolve to escalate further if necessary — but doing so well below the ultimate deterrence threat of societal destruction. That "ultimate threat" could be held in reserve to help ensure that the opponent would continue to have an overwhelming incentive *not* to further escalate a conflict for fear of unleashing unlimited nuclear destruction: "The [U.S.] risk involved in a bit of less-than-massive retaliation would be a good deal less than it is now because the fear of an all-out [Soviet] strike in return should be a good deal less...the [U.S.] threat of limited retaliation (even on a scale that deserves the word 'massive') would become a great deal more credible."[57]

This rationale for limited nuclear threats also does *not* presume that a "limited" nuclear war could be fought safely or with any certainty that a limited war would remain limited in any meaningful sense. It also is *not* an endorsement of nuclear "war-fighting." Rather, the existence of graduated options is intended to contribute *to both the initial deterrence of limited attacks* and the reestablishment of deterrence ("intra-war deterrence") to bound escalation following a limited attack. Brandishing limited nuclear response options and thereby demonstrating resolve for these deterrence purposes has been an apparent feature of declared U.S. deterrence policy since the mid-1970s.[58] As then-Secretary of Defense James

---

[57] Schelling, "Surprise Attack and Disarmament," op. cit., p. 207.

[58] In 1974, Secretary of Defense James Schlesinger observed that all previous planned U.S. options involved "literally thousands of weapons" and emphasized the need for limited nuclear response options. He announced publicly that the United States would introduce limited nuclear threat options to provide greater credibility for the deterrence of limited threats. He said this was made necessary because increased Soviet nuclear capabilities had rendered the credibility of large-scale US response options to limited attacks "close to zero." See, James Schlesinger, *US/USS.R. Strategic Policies*, Testimony in, US Senate, Committee on Foreign Relations, 93rd Congress, 2nd Session, March 4,

Schlesinger observed, "To the extent that we have selective response options — smaller and more precisely focused than in the past — we should be able to deter such challenges. But if deterrence fails, we may be able to bring all but the largest nuclear conflicts to a rapid conclusion before cities are struck. Damage may thus be limited and further escalation avoided."[59] The Department of Defense specified publicly at that time that the targets for a limited response could include hardened missile silos, soft military targets such as airfields, and (or) cities.[60] The requirement for graduated response options to help deter limited threats and limit escalation if deterrence fails is emphasized most recently in the Defense Department's 2018 *Nuclear Posture Review*.[61]

The capacity to issue graduated nuclear threats does not necessarily create a corresponding requirement for much-increased nuclear forces beyond the numbers otherwise considered necessary for deterrence. It does necessitate the manifest planning and control of forces that enable graduated threats to be made known to opponents for these deterrence purposes.[62]

1974, p. 9, see also, pp. 7, 12-13, 55. James Schlesinger, *Annual Defense Department Report, FY 1976 and FY 197T* (Washington, D.C.: USGPO, February 5, 1975), p. II-3-II-4; and, James Schlesinger, *Annual Defense Department Report FY 1975* (Washington, D.C.: USGPO, March 4, 1974), pp. 32, 42.

[59] Schlesinger, *Annual Defense Department Report FY 1975*, op. cit., p. 38.

[60] Ibid., p. 39.

[61] Office of the Secretary of Defense, *Nuclear Posture Review* (February 2018), pp. 52-55.

[62] Secretary of Defense Schlesinger emphasized that capability for limited nuclear response options required no increase in the number of nuclear weapons, but did require the planning and control necessary for limited strike options. See, Schlesinger, *U.S./U.S.S.R. Strategic Policies*, op. cit., p. 17; and Schlesinger, *Annual Defense Department Report FY 1975*, op. cit., p. 44.

Uncertainty Deters

The easy deterrence narrative typically includes another "extra-Realist" expectation about the functioning of deterrence that facilitates the conclusion that deterrence is easy and reliable. This second expectation is that opponents' *uncertainty* about whether, when and how the United States actually would execute its nuclear threat can provide *adequate credibility* for effective deterrence. An opponent's uncertainty about whether the deterrent threat would be executed following its provocation can deter its attack because the consequences would be so catastrophic if executed: "Uncertainty of response, not certainty, is required for deterrence because, if retaliation occurs, one risks losing so much."[63] Thomas Schelling posited that the credibility of nuclear deterrence depends *not* on an opponent's certainty that nuclear catastrophe would follow its highly-aggressive action, but on the "*chance*" that catastrophe would follow. Schelling famously called this, "the [deterrence] threat that leaves something to chance."[64]

Early in the Cold War, Schelling explained why uncertain nuclear threats are sufficient to deter in a balance of terror: "Any situation that scares one side will scare both sides with the danger of a war that neither wants, and both will have to pick their way carefully through the crisis, never sure that the other knows how to avoid stumbling over the brink."[65]

Waltz concurred: "In a conventional world, a country can sensibly attack if it believes that success is probable. In a nuclear world, a country cannot sensibly attack unless it believes that success is assured. An attacker is deterred even

---

[63] Waltz in, Sagan and Waltz, op. cit., p. 24.

[64] See in particular, Schelling, *The Strategy of Conflict*, op. cit., Chapter 8.

[65] Schelling, *Arms and Influence*, op. cit., p. 99.

if he believes only that the attacked may retaliate."[66] The possibility or "chance" of such loss provides adequate deterrence because, "A low probability of carrying a highly destructive attack home is sufficient for deterrence."[67]

According to this easy deterrence narrative, the expectation that the *chance* that the United States would execute its nuclear deterrent is adequate for deterrence is particularly important to the integrity of America's extended nuclear deterrence "umbrella" to allies. It answers the concern that America's deterrent threat of employing nuclear weapons in defense of allies should be seen as an unconvincing bluff, not an effective deterrent, *because doing so could easily result in the destruction of the United States.* During the Cold War, the proposition that the United States would *likely not prove willing* to employ nuclear weapons on behalf of allies because the ultimate consequences would be intolerable for Washington seemed to undercut fatally the U.S. extended nuclear deterrent for allies (i.e., the United States would not prove willing to "trade New York for Berlin"). This concern was likely exacerbated by the comments of some U.S. officials (once out of office) seemingly acknowledging that the U.S. extended nuclear deterrent should be discounted as a bluff.[68]

---

[66] Waltz, "The Spread of Nuclear Weapons: More May be Better," op. cit.

[67] Waltz, "The Spread of Nuclear Weapons: More May be Better," op. cit.; Professor Robert Jervis makes the same claim: "Even a very small probability of escalation is sufficient to deter serious encroachments." Jervis, "Why Nuclear Superiority Doesn't Matter," op. cit., p. 619.

[68] In 1979, Henry Kissinger remarked publicly that, "Our European allies should not keep asking us to multiply strategic assurances that we cannot possibly mean, or if we do mean, we should not want to execute, because if we execute, we risk the destruction of civilization." Henry Kissinger, "The Future of NATO," in, *NATO, The Next Thirty Years,* Kenneth Myers, ed. (Boulder, CO: Westview Press, 1981), p. 8.

However, the easy deterrence narrative's expectation that an *uncertain* U.S. threat is sufficient for extended nuclear deterrence mitigates this concern. Extended deterrence *can* work, even if U.S. execution of the threat would be self-destructive because the opponent *could never discount the "chance" that the United States would execute its deterrent threat* by way of an irrational act or the fog of war;[69] that chance is adequate to deter. Consequently, the seemingly innocuous proposition that uncertain nuclear threats can deter reliably plays a central role in the easy deterrence narrative, particularly for extended deterrence.

This contention that deterrence can be based on an opponent's uncertainty regarding the U.S. nuclear deterrence threat was prominent in both academic discourse and official policy statements during the Cold War,[70] and again remains a theme in public discussions. It contributes significantly to defining "how much is enough?" for deterrence in terms that are easily achieved and sustained. How so? It means that effective deterrence does *not* require that the country attempting to deter *convince* opponents that it would, in fact, deliberately, rationally execute its nuclear deterrent threat if provoked. The country seeking to deter can forego those offensive or defensive strategic capabilities, or potentially provocative declarations that might otherwise be thought necessary to *fully convince* opponents of the certainty of its deterrence threat, i.e., that it surely would be executed as threatened. The easy deterrence narrative contends that such additional requirements are unnecessary for deterrence because threat credibility with that sense of certainty is unnecessary for deterrence.

---

[69] Thomas Schelling elaborated this proposition that uncertainty deters in some detail. See the discussion in, Keith Payne, *The Great American Gamble* (Fairfax, VA: National Institute Press, 2008), pp, 31-35.

[70] See the discussion in Ibid., pp. 91-96.

In short, not only are the required second-strike nuclear forces modest and thus easily acquired, but additional strategic capabilities *are unnecessary to convince opponents of the logical credibility of the threat.*   The easy deterrence narrative reaches these sanguine conclusions about the reliability and ease of deterrence via this combination of several basic Realist assumptions about leadership decision-making and the "extra-Realist" expectations that deterrence can be based on *uncertain threats to the opponent's societal assets.*

Easy Deterrence: No "Ironclad" Guarantees, but Reasons for Optimism

This narrative leads to considerable optimism about the ease and predictability of deterrence.   Indeed, as noted above, some government officials and academics have attributed near-certainty to its reliability. However, others acknowledge that deterrence is not foolproof. For example, Waltz observes that the deterrence stability compelled by the need for mutual restraint is *not* guaranteed. It could be upended by leaders who are not "sensible:"   "A small number system can always be disrupted by the actions of a Hitler and the reactions of a Chamberlain."[71]   Jervis elaborates on why this is so: "Miscalculations are possible, even in situations that seem very clear in retrospect, and states are sometimes willing to take what others think are exorbitant risks to try to reach highly valued goals."[72] Brodie adds simply that, "The leaders of no nation will wish to risk the total destruction of their country....But what if

---

[71] Kenneth Waltz, *Theory of International Politics* (Boston: McGraw Hill, 1979), p. 175.

[72] Jervis, "Why Nuclear Superiority Doesn't Matter," op. cit., p. 633.

another Hitler comes along?....We should not complain too much because the guarantee is not ironclad."[73]

Despite this caveat regarding deterrence that "nothing in this world is certain,"[74] considerable "comfort" and "cautious optimism" are warranted with regard to the reliability of deterrence — not because leaders are reliably virtuous, but because the dangers involved in reckless behavior are so obvious (the "crystal ball effect"): "With nuclear weapons, it's been proven without exception that whoever gets nuclear weapons behaves with caution and moderation. Every country — whether they are countries we trust and think of as being highly responsible, like Britain, or countries we distrust greatly for very good reasons, like China during the Cultural Revolution — behaves with such caution."[75]

In addition, even if an individual leader is reckless, "those who direct the activities of great states are by no means free agents."[76] There may be a variety of pressures contributing to sensible behavior that are beyond the character of a particular leader or leadership, including the possible refusal of those who carry out orders to engage in reckless actions in the face of nuclear threat. As 2007 Nobel Laureate Professor Roger Myerson says in this regard: "Our most dangerous adversaries are not lone madmen, however, but are leaders with political support from many people who have normal hopes and fears. Psychopathic militarists like Hitler become a threat to our civilization only

---

[73] Brodie, *War and Politics*, op. cit., p. 403, 430.

[74] Waltz in, Sagan and Waltz, op. cit., p. 126.

[75] Kenneth Waltz, in Scott Sagan, Kenneth Waltz and Richard Betts, "A Nuclear Iran: Promoting Stability or Courting Disaster?" *Journal of International Affairs*, Vol. 60, No. 2 (Spring/Summer 2007), p.137. (Transcript of a debate between Waltz and Sagan, Kellogg Conference Center, Columbia University School of International and Public Affairs, February 8, 2007).

[76] Waltz, *Theory of International Politics*, op. cit., p. 176.

when ordinary rational people become motivated to support them as leaders."[77] For nuclear deterrence in a proper balance of terror to fail, "One would have to believe that a whole set of leaders might suddenly go mad."[78] Brodie adds: "We have ample reason to feel now that nuclear weapons do act critically to deter wars between the major powers, and not nuclear wars alone but any wars."[79]

Also, as noted earlier, the absence of war among great powers since the end of World War II suggests the predictable reliability of nuclear deterrence: "Never since the Treaty of Westphalia in 1648...have great powers enjoyed a longer period of peace than we have known since the Second World War. One can scarcely believe that the presence of nuclear weapons does not greatly help to explain this happy condition."[80] This extraordinary history, according to Waltz, argues *against* the expectation that nuclear deterrence is likely to fail. Indeed, he finds it "odd" that, "a happy nuclear past leads many to expect an unhappy nuclear future."[81]

Finally, this narrative includes the expectation that if deterrence fails at some point, graduated nuclear options and intra-war deterrence could help prevent its escalation. While there are no guarantees, "even if deterrence should fail, the prospects for rapid de-escalation are good."[82]

---

[77] Roger B. Myerson, *Force and Restraint in Strategic Deterrence: A Game-Theorist's Perspective* (Carlisle, PA: U.S. Army War College, Strategic Studies Institute, November 2007), p. 22.

[78] Waltz, "Nuclear Myths and Political Realities," op. cit., p. 737.

[79] Brodie, *War and Politics*, op. cit., p. 430.

[80] Waltz, "Nuclear Myths and Political Realities," op. cit., p. 744.

[81] Waltz, "The Spread of Nuclear Weapons: More May be Better," op. cit.

[82] Waltz, "The Spread of Nuclear Weapons: More May Be Better," op. cit.; see also, Schelling, *The Strategy of Conflict*, op. cit., p. 253.

Strategic Force Recommendations from This Easy Deterrence Narrative

The force recommendations that follow from the easy deterrence narrative focus on the need for survivable nuclear capabilities that *are able* to hold an opponent's societal assets at risk, but *are not able to threaten the opponent's own deterrence forces*. Why this balance? Because stable deterrence follows from the ability to threaten the opponent's societal assets, but a capability to threaten the opponent's own deterrence forces is not consistent with a stable *mutual* balance of terror. Offensive forces able to strike an opponent's deterrence forces on the ground, or air defenses, ballistic missile defenses or civil defenses intended to protect cities against the opponent's bomber and missile capabilities are unnecessary for deterrence and would threaten to upset stability by calling into question the opponent's deterrence capability. Why so? Because such forces could cause an opponent to doubt the effectiveness of its deterrent and thus drive the opponent to move in haste to gain the possible advantage of striking first rather than waiting to absorb an initial undeterred blow.

Colin S. Gray explains the easy deterrence narrative's logic against defensive capabilities: "Because mutual vulnerability is considered the ultimate basis for deterrence stability, neither nation should seek to acquire the means physically to limit damage to its homeland, through active and passive defenses or through development of offensive forces that threaten the survivability of the strategic retaliatory forces of the other side."[83] Offensive or defensive forces that might threaten the pre- or post-launch survivability of an opponent's deterrence forces could in this way create what Schelling called, "the reciprocal fear of

---

[83] Gray, *Nuclear Strategy and Strategic Planning* (Philadelphia: Foreign Policy Research Institute, 1984), p. 68.

surprise attack."[84] This fear, according to Schelling, is one of very few routes to war imaginable in the context of a balance of terror: "It is hard to imagine how anybody would be precipitated into full-scale war by accident, false alarm, mischief, or momentary panic, if it were not for such urgency to get in quick."[85] Mitigating this possible "fear of surprise attack" by avoiding "destabilizing" forces provides reliable deterrence because, "The *likelihood* of war is determined by how great a reward attaches to jumping the gun, how strong the incentive to hedge against war itself by starting it, how great the penalty on giving peace the benefit of the doubt in a crisis;"[86] and, "If the advantage of striking first can be eliminated or severely reduced, the incentive to strike at all will be reduced."[87]

Consequently, the easy deterrence narrative's general guidelines for stable deterrence typically *favor* the survivable, modest offensive capabilities needed to threaten societal assets, which could include "targets that are crucial to a nation's modern economy, for example, electrical, oil, and energy nodes, and transportation hubs."[88] However, the same guidelines *argue against: 1)* offensive nuclear systems able to threaten the pre-launch survivability of an opponent's own deterrence forces; and 2) strategic defensive capabilities designed to physically protect one's own society.   These two types of capabilities, while defensive in intent, are "destabilizing" because they could undermine an opponent's confidence in its deterrence

---

[84] Schelling, *The Strategy of Conflict*, op. cit., pp. 207-229.

[85] Schelling, *Arms and Influence*, op. cit., p. 227.

[86] Schelling, *Arms and Influence*, op. cit., p. 285. (Emphasis in original).

[87] Schelling, *The Strategy of Conflict*, op. cit., p. 231.

[88] Hans M. Kristensen, Robert S. Norris, Ivan Oelrich, *From Counterforce to Minimal Deterrence: A New Nuclear Policy on the Path Toward Eliminating Nuclear Weapons* (Washington, D.C.: Federation of American Scientists and the National Resources Defense Council, April 2009), pp. 31-32.

capabilities thus triggering the "reciprocal fear of surprise attack" and a hasty road to war.[89] The concern that strategic defenses could destabilize deterrence has been a prominent theme for decades in much of the public commentary and some official policy statements.[90]

Confidence in the reliable working of deterrence also contributed to the conclusion that attempting to physically protect society against strategic nuclear attack not only is unnecessary for deterrence and potentially destabilizing, but also is of limited potential value because a stable balance of terror provides reliable protection via deterrence — and does so *in the absence of such defenses*. Waltz summarizes this prevalent view with the concise rhetorical question, "Why should anyone want to replace stable deterrence with unstable defense?,"[91] and, "In a nuclear world defensive systems are predictably destabilizing. It would be folly to move from a condition of stable deterrence to one of

---

[89] Schelling, *The Strategy of Conflict*, op. cit., p. 233.

[90] Former Secretary of Defense Harold Brown made this point with remarkable clarity in his fiscal year 1980 annual Department of Defense report: "*In the interests of [deterrence] stability, we avoid the capability of eliminating the other side's deterrent,* insofar as we might be able to do so. In short, we must be quite willing — as we have been for some time — to accept the principle of mutual deterrence, and design our defense posture in light of that principle." Harold Brown, *Department of Defense Annual Report Fiscal Year 1980* (Washington, D.C.: USGPO, 1979), p. 61. (Emphasis added). See also, Statement of Paul Warnke in, U.S. Senate, Committee on Banking, Housing and Urban Affairs, *Civil Defense,* Hearings, 95th Congress, 2nd Session (Washington, D.C.: USGPO, 1979), p. 4; and, Henry S. Rowen, "Formulating Strategic Doctrine," Commission on the Organization of the Government for the Conduct of Foreign Policy, Volume 4, Appendix K, *Adequacy of Current Organization: Defense and Arms Control* (Washington, D.C.: USGPO, June 1975), p. 228. More recently see, Department of Defense, *Ballistic Missile Defense Review Report* (February 2010), pp. 12-13.

[91] Waltz in, Sagan and Waltz, *The Spread of Nuclear Weapons: A Debate Renewed*, op. cit., p. 153.

unstable defense."[92]   During the Cold War, Secretary McNamara largely rejected strategic defenses against the Soviet Union given his confidence in deterrence, and because he concluded that defenses could not be sufficiently effective to provide "meaningful" protection for Americans given likely Soviet countermeasures: "Until there are inventions that have not yet even been imagined, a defense robust and cheap enough to replace deterrence will remain a pipe dream."[93]

In short, based initially on several traditional points of Realist thought and perhaps more importantly on the "extra-Realist" elaborations described above, early in the Cold War prominent academics and officials developed a compelling and comforting deterrence narrative that posits the ease and efficacy of a balance of terror to prevent nuclear or large-scale conventional war.   The expected ease and efficacy follow from: the basic Realist tenets that countries generally act rationally and seek as a priority to preserve national survival; the relatively modest nuclear forces needed to threaten opponents' societal assets; the expectation that even uncertain threats will serve to deter reliably; and the conviction that attempting to physically protect society against attack is unnecessary and largely undesirable.   The offensive and defensive force requirements following from this narrative are relatively modest and narrow.

U.S. policy never followed this easy deterrence narrative in its entirety, and official public characterizations of U.S. deterrence requirements became increasingly distant beginning in the mid-1970s. However, the easy deterrence narrative's modest and narrow force requirements for a stable balance of terror and related basic arguments against

---

[92] Waltz, "Nuclear Myths and Political Realities," op. cit., p. 743.

[93] Robert S. McNamara, *Blundering Into Disaster: Surviving the First Century of the Nuclear Age* (New York: Pantheon Books, 1986), p. 95. See also, Payne, *The Great American Gamble*, op. cit., pp. 108-119.

"destabilizing" strategic offensive and defensive capabilities were and continue to be prominent themes in the U.S. public debate about deterrence and force requirements. They have been particularly helpful arguments for strategic nuclear force limits and reductions. In 1965, referring to this narrative as "Finite Deterrence," Herman Kahn observed: "Finite Deterrence seems compatible with all kinds of measures for arms control...In particular, Finite Deterrence is compatible with 'parity,' nuclear stalemates, a 'no first use of nuclear weapons' doctrine, a 'no first strike' doctrine, and other attempts to achieve limits and stability. And to the extent that one viewed the situation as a kind of spiraling arms race trap in which the Americans and Soviets were involuntarily caught, this was a way to get out of it."[94] Indeed, this sanguine deterrence narrative has been the primary basis for the argument that U.S. nuclear forces can be reduced deeply because "overkill" is unnecessary and can be discarded or negotiated away without undermining deterrence. It also has been the basis for arguments to limit offensive and defensive strategic forces that might appear capable of threatening the other's nuclear arsenal because they are unnecessary and potentially destabilizing. These arguments together have played in virtually every public debate about U.S.-Soviet and U.S.-Russian strategic nuclear arms control initiatives since the late 1960s — perhaps most obviously in favor of the 1972 Anti-Ballistic Missile (ABM) Treaty limiting strategic missile defenses and in near-continuous U.S. attempts to limit large ICBMs that can threaten the other's nuclear retaliatory forces.[95]

---

[94] Herman Kahn, "United States Central War Policy," in Robert Goldwin, ed., *Beyond the Cold War* (Chicago: Rand McNally, 1966), p. 48.

[95] As described by senior Clinton Administration officials John Deutch and James Woolsey, and Brent Scowcroft, National Security Advisor to Presidents Ford and George H.W. Bush. See Brent Scowcroft, John

An Alternative Deterrence Narrative: No Easy Deterrence

Some disarmament proponents approvingly describe adopting the easy deterrence narrative as policy to be a useful "transitional" step "on the path toward nuclear zero."[96] Nevertheless, there is obvious friction between this deterrence narrative and the Idealist nuclear disarmament agenda.[97]   The former posits an extremely valuable continuing role for nuclear weapons and endorses maintaining some nuclear capabilities for stable deterrence. In contrast, the disarmament agenda often is extremely critical of nuclear deterrence as being inherently unsound and dangerous, and seeks to stigmatize nuclear weapons and establish a global norm against them to advance their elimination.   The envisaged policy priorities and foreseeable endpoints are mutually exclusive. Indeed, as noted in Chapter 1, Brodie refers to the value of nuclear deterrence as a "very great gain," and concludes that "We should no doubt be hesitant about relinquishing it even if we could."[98]   Schelling emphasized the great difference between his favored approach to arms control as a means to

---

Deutch, and R. James Woolsey, "A Small, Survivable, Mobile ICBM," *Washington Post*, December 26, 1986, p. A23.

[96] Kristensen, Norris, and Oelrich, op. cit., p. 31.

[97] For example, even while generally supporting reductions and limitations on nuclear arms, Michael Krepon emphasizes that "a safe global nuclear order" includes nuclear deterrence. See, Michael Krepon, "Trump's Track Record of Nuclear Deterrence Without Reassurance Is Dangerous," *Forbes Online*, November 25, 2019, available at https://www.forbes.com/sites/michaelkrepon/2019/11/25/trumps-track-record-of-nuclear-deterrence-without-reassurance-is-dangerous/#1274e33d518a.

[98] Brodie, *War and Politics*, op. cit., p. 430.

codify a *nuclear balance of terror for deterrence* and "the 'ban the bomb' orientation."[99]

During the Cold War a largely separate set of prominent academics and scholars developed a markedly different nuclear deterrence narrative that, like the Idealist disarmament agenda, has considerable friction with the easy deterrence narrative — but largely for different reasons. This alternative narrative certainly concurs that deterrence is valuable, even necessary for the United States in an anarchic international system. It includes some variation among its authors and has evolved over decades. However, in sharp contrast to the easy deterrence narrative derived from points elaborated by Schelling, Waltz and Brodie, and Jervis, this alternative narrative envisages deterrence as *difficult* to establish and sustain, and as potentially demanding considerably greater nuclear capabilities, contingency planning and, for some, strategic defensive capabilities. Correspondingly, its general force guidelines are quite different from those of the easy deterrence narrative.

This alternative difficult deterrence narrative first emerged early in the Cold War — at least in part in response to the inadequacies other scholars saw in the sanguine easy deterrence narrative. They included most prominently Herman Kahn and Albert Wohlstetter, both of the RAND Corporation at the time, and more recently, Colin Gray. For example, Wohlstetter began his famous 1958 article, *The Delicate Balance of Terror*, with the following: "I should like to examine the stability of the thermonuclear balance which, it is generally supposed, would make aggression irrational or even insane. The balance, I believe, is in fact precarious, and this fact has critical implications for policy. Deterrence in the 1960's will be neither inevitable nor impossible but the product of sustained intelligent effort, attainable only by

---

[99] Schelling, *The Strategy of Conflict*, op. cit., p. 241.

continuing hard choice...While feasible, it will be much harder to achieve in the 1960's than is generally believed. One of the most disturbing features of current opinion is the underestimation of this difficulty."[100]   This classic early work captured much of the basic criticism of the easy deterrence narrative and points toward a competing deterrence narrative derived in succeeding years from the works of Wohlstetter, Kahn, Gray and others.

Bernard Brodie's commentary on Wohlstetter's contention of a "delicate balance of terror" illustrates a fundamental disagreement between these two competing deterrence narratives: "I could never accept the implications of [Wohlstetter's] title — that the balance of terror between the Soviet Union and the United States ever has been or ever could be 'delicate.' My reasons have to do mostly with human inhibitions against taking monumental risks or doing things which are universally detested..."[101] Brodie's comment demonstrates that while both approaches to deterrence have some Realist origins, they posit: 1) strikingly different expectations about leadership decision-making and behavior; 2) different expectations about the functioning of deterrence; and, 3) correspondingly, different answers to the question "how much is enough?" for deterrence.   These two different basic narratives have, on occasion, been attributed to their respective authors' deterrence optimism or pessimism. That labeling, however, is somewhat misleading: the easy deterrence narrative does *not* contend that deterrence will always "work," and the alternative difficult deterrence narrative does not contend that it must fail. Rather, *the difference in perspectives is more about differing expectations about the plausible range of opponent*

[100] Albert Wohlstetter, *The Delicate Balance of Terror*, Document P-1472, The RAND Corporation, 1958, at
https://www.rand.org/pubs/papers/P1472.html.

[101] Bernard Brodie, "The Development of Nuclear Strategy," *International Security*, Vol. 2, No. 4 (Spring 1978), p. 69.

decision-making and behavior, and the corresponding ease or difficulty of identifying and meeting the requirements for deterrence.

Both of these deterrence narratives consider nuclear deterrence valuable and even essential for U.S. and allied security — at least for some time. However, in contrast to the easy deterrence narrative, this alternative difficult deterrence narrative sees the pursuit of deterrence as an ongoing and difficult challenge, with no fixed approach and no corresponding finite and fixed set of nuclear capabilities that can predictably provide the desired deterrent effects.

For example, as noted above, the easy deterrence narrative has considerable confidence that all rational or sensible leaders will respond with predictable prudence and caution when confronted with the "chance" that the nuclear destruction of their society could follow from their highly provocative move. In contrast, the difficult deterrence narrative posits that such an expectation may be a "fatal error," not simply because leaders might be irrational, but because: "Not all actors in international politics calculate utility in making decisions in the same way. Differences in values, culture, attitudes toward risk-taking, and so on vary greatly. There is no substitute for knowledge of the adversary's mind-set and behavioral style, and this is often difficult to obtain or to apply correctly in assessing intentions or predicting responses."[102] In short, rational leadership decision-making can vary greatly and unique decision-making factors can drive leaders' perceptions and calculations of value, cost and risk in surprising, unpredictable directions. Consequently, the functioning of deterrence "is heavily context dependent."[103]

---

[102] Gordon A. Craig, Alexander L. George, *Force and Statecraft: Diplomatic Problems of Our Time*, Third Edition (New York: Oxford University Press, 1995), p. 188.

[103] Ibid., p. 192.

During the Cold War, Colin Gray pointed to the variability in leadership perceptions and calculations in his full rejection of the easy deterrence narrative: "Assessments of the stability of deterrence err because they do not take account" of differences in "political will" and leadership perceptions/values. For example, "Sensitivity to human loss has not been a prominent feature of Soviet (or Russian) political culture. Anyone who believes that nuclear war should mean the same to Americans and to Great Russians should reflect deeply on the contrasting histories of the two societies." As a result of this type of variability, "there is massive uncertainty over 'what deters' (who? on what issue? when?)."[104] Uncertainty pertains to all defense planning, and presents deterrence planners with an incomplete basis for prediction "no matter how cunning their methodology or polished their crystal ball."[105]

The confident expectation of an opponent's sensible prudence and caution when presented with a severe societal deterrence threat may be upset by a variety of factors that can affect a rational opponent's decision-making, and which may not be obvious in advance to an outside observer. These factors may include, for example: an opponent's hierarchy of values that posits an expectation of *intolerable cost* associated with *not* acting, or an unwillingness to yield to a societal deterrence threat; an opponent's willingness to take great risks in unwavering pursuit of a cherished goal that demands highly provocative behavior; an opponent's confidence that it need not conciliate because the deterrer itself will yield in a confrontation and/or that it is protected from the deterrer's threat, including by divine power; an opponent's unwillingness or inability to recognize great risk; and, the

---

[104] Colin Gray, *Nuclear Strategy and Strategic Planning*, op. cit., pp. 46, 47, 64.

[105] Colin S. Gray, *Strategy and Defence Planning: Meeting the Challenge of Uncertainty* (London: Oxford University Press, 2014), p. 1.

interference of unexpected technical, operational, and organizational factors in the implementation of the hoped-for prudent leadership decision-making.[106]   Historical examples suggest that each of these dynamics, and more, can interfere with the predictable functioning of deterrence.[107]   A 2014 study by the National Research Council of the National Academy of Sciences emphasizes that taking account of such factors is critical in considerations of deterrence.[108]

The late Oxford University professor Robert O'Neill captured a consequence of these factors — some leadership calculations and choices may be inexplicable, and even appear irrational because: "Many of those who initiate wars either do not understand what they are doing or fail to realize the size of the gamble they are taking."[109]   An examination of multiple international crises puts the matter more pointedly: "The personality of an individual determines the reaction to information and events.   A leader's nationality, passion, idealism, cynicism, pragmatism, dogmatism, stupidity, intelligence, imagination, flexibility, stubbornness, and so on, along with

---

[106] For a thorough discussion of this final organizational factor interfering with the predictable functioning of deterrence see, Scott Sagan in, Sagan and Waltz, *The Spread of Nuclear Weapons: A Debate Renewed*, op. cit., pp. 46-87.

[107] Historical examples of these types of factors affecting leadership decision-making in unexpected ways are presented in, Keith Payne, *Deterrence in the Second Nuclear Age* (Lexington, KY: University Press of Kentucky, 1996), pp. 79-119; see also, Keith Payne, *The Fallacies of Cold War Deterrence and a New Direction* (Lexington, KY: University Press of Kentucky, 2001), pp. 1-77.

[108] National Research Council, *U.S. Air Force Deterrence Analytic Capabilities* (Washington, D.C.: National Academies Press, 2014), pp. 35-39, 93-95.

[109] Robert O'Neill, "The Use of Military Force: Constant Factors and New Trends," *The Changing Strategic Landscape*, Part II, in *Adelphi Papers*, No. 236 (London: International Institute for Strategic Studies, 1989), p. 3.

mental disorders such as depression, anxiety, and paranoia, shape reactions and decisions during a crisis."[110]   Indeed, advancements in cognitive science have demonstrated the significant degree to which decision-making often is governed not only by prudent cost-benefit calculations, but by many possible less predictable factors, including emotion and cognitive biases such as confirmation bias, optimism bias, survivorship bias, and normalcy bias.[111]

In any confrontation opposing leaders may be highly or hardly motivated, cautious or incautious, methodical or impulsive, pragmatic or obsessively driven, attentive or distant, and highly constrained by their political circumstances or free to follow their own possibly eccentric wills and psyches. Consequently, the difficult and easy deterrence narratives diverge sharply because they do not share the expectation that the "crystal ball effect" will reliably mitigate all such inherently human decision-making factors and thereby ensure caution and prudence in response to even severe deterrence threats. Indeed, because deterrence is vulnerable to "mismanagement," Herman Kahn and Colin Gray deemed long-term reliance on nuclear deterrence to preserve peace to be "foolish" if a more benign alternative were available.[112]

---

[110] Jonathan Roberts, *Decision-Making during International Crises* (New York: St. Martin's Press, 1988), pp. 162-163.

[111] For a recent concise summary of this point and some of its implications for deterrence see, Lain King, "What Do Cognitive Biases Mean for Deterrence?" February 12, 2019, available at, https://thestrategybridge.org/the-bridge/2019/2/12/what-do-cognitive-biases-mean-for-deterrence. See also, Thomas Scheber, "Evolutionary Psychology: Cognitive Function, and Deterrence," in *Understanding Deterrence*, Keith B. Payne, ed. (New York: Routledge, 2013), pp. 65-92.

[112] Gray, *Nuclear Strategy and Strategic Planning*, op. cit., pp. 88, 92; Herman Kahn, *The Nature and Feasibility of War and Deterrence*, P-1888-RC (Santa Monica: The RAND Corporation, January 20, 1961), pp. 40, 46.

While other prominent scholars including Waltz, Jervis, and Brodie clearly recognized the potential for variation in cognition and decision-making and that deterrence is not "ironclad," it is the difficult deterrence narrative that is much more shaped by its potentially distorting effects on the predictable functioning of and requirements for deterrence. As noted, this variability can stem from a variety of potential deeply human factors affecting different leaderships uniquely, including their respective cognitive biases, "values, culture, and attitudes toward risk-taking."

Numerous analyses of historical case studies conclude that these types of factors can affect leadership decision-making and thus the functioning of deterrence. For example, as one noted inductive study concludes in this regard:

> Even the most elaborate efforts to demonstrate prowess and resolve [for deterrence] may prove insufficient to discourage a challenge when policy makers are attracted to a policy of brinkmanship as a necessary means of preserving vital strategic and domestic political interests....These cases and others point to the importance of motivation as the key to brinkmanship challenges. To the extent that leaders perceive the need to act, they become insensitive to the interests and commitments of others that stand in the way of the success of their policy.[113]

Consequently, expectations of how deterrence "should" work with "sensible" leaders must take into account that many factors may shape leadership decision-making/behavior in unpredictable directions. Alexander

---

[113] Richard Ned Lebow, "The Deterrence Deadlock: Is There a Way Out?" in Robert Jervis, Richard Ned Lebow, and Janice Gross Stein, *Psychology & Deterrence* (Baltimore: Johns Hopkins University Press, 1985), p. 183.

George and Richard Smoke recognized this variability in a conclusion of their classic examination of deterrence, *Deterrence in American Foreign Policy: Theory and Practice*: "Substantively, deterrence theory is seriously incomplete, to say the least, for a normative-prescriptive application."[114] This point regarding the variability of leadership decision-making is the antithesis of the apparent "mirror imaging" of easy deterrence, and its implications for deterrence considerations contrast sharply with the sanguine expectation that state leaders can be expected to respond to a severe punitive deterrence threat with prudence, caution and pragmatism.

Implications of Variation in Decision-Making: No Easy Deterrence

A reliably effective deterrent threat must overcome the possibly wide variation in opponents' perceptions, calculations and decision-making. The implications of this seemingly academic point for deterrence are enormous. Because the definition of what constitutes "sensible" leadership thinking and behavior can vary greatly, generalized expectations of how easily deterrence *should* function and the finite forces that *should* reliably deter may be misleading at best for any specific case. As the noted British scholar Sir Lawrence Freedman concludes with regard to confident predictions about the functioning of deterrence: "To come up with propositions about when, in particular conditions certain types of deterrence are more or less likely to work" may be an interesting intellectual exercise, "but practitioners may find it frustrating, as it provides little reliable guidance for policy other than to

---

[114] Alexander George and Richard Smoke, *Deterrence in American Foreign Policy: Theory and Practice* (New York: Columbia University Press, 1974), p. 83.

suggest that close attention [be] paid to the specifics of a situation..."[115]

For example, one consequence of this variation in decision-making is the likelihood that different leaderships will place highest priority on different possible values, national or personal. The easy deterrence narrative's expectation that leaders will reliably place highest value on the preservation of their country's societal infrastructure and thus should be deterred predictably via punitive nuclear threats to societal targets may often be accurate. But history demonstrates conclusively that leaders can place priority on other/different values, some material and others intangible, and this prioritization can shape their decision-making. Several very brief examples illustrate this point. Together, they demonstrate how leadership decision-making can be driven by a variety of priorities and motivations that may defy easy prediction—potentially dashing confident expectations of how deterrence *should* function if leaders are sensible.

In 1945, following the atomic attacks on Hiroshima and Nagasaki, the Japanese War Minister, Korechika Anami, and Navy Chief of Staff, Toyoda Soemu, in apparent deference to their concepts of national honor, sought the continuation of the war even if it meant the destruction of Japan.[116]

In 1958, Mao Zedong ordered a massive shelling of the small island of Quemoy for the purpose of eliciting U.S. nuclear threats. He later wrote to Soviet leader Nikita Khrushchev that he, "would be only too happy for China to

---

[115] Lawrence Freedman, *Deterrence* (Malden, MA: Polity Press, 2004), p. 117.

[116] See the discussion in David McCullough, *Truman* (New York: Simon and Schuster, 1992), p. 459. See also, Edwin P. Hoyt, *Japan's War: The Great Pacific Conflict* (New York: Cooper Square Press, 2001), pp. 402-403; and, Thomas R. Flagel, *The History Buff's Guide to World War II* (Naperville, IL: Cumberland House, 2012), pp. 240-241.

fight a nuclear war with America alone. 'For our ultimate victory,' he offered, 'for the total eradication of the imperialists, we are willing to endure the first strike. All it is is a big pile of people dying.'"[117]

In 1962, Nikita Khrushchev moved nuclear weapons to Cuba despite his expectation that, as a consequence, "they can attack us and we shall respond. This may end in a big war."[118] During the same crisis and in an expression of socialist ideological zeal, Cuban leaders apparently urged Soviet leaders to launch a nuclear attack against the United States despite their recognition that the consequences would be a horrific war and the destruction of Cuba.[119]

Finally, in October 1973, Egypt and Syria launched a massive armored attack against Israel to restore national honor despite the purported possibility of Israeli nuclear retaliation.[120] U.S. leaders were surprised by this large-scale attack on Israel and the Yom Kippur War because, according to then-Secretary of State Henry Kissinger, "Our definition of rationality did not take seriously the notion of [Egypt and Syria] starting an unwinnable war to restore self-respect.   There was no defense against our own preconceptions."[121] The Egyptian and Syrian leaderships'

---

[117]Quoted in, Jung Chang and Jon Halliday, *Mao: The Unknown Story* (New York: Alfred Knopf, 2005), pp. 413-414.

[118] Quoted in, Aleksander Fursenko and Timothy Naftali, *One Hell of a Gamble: Khrushchev, Castro and Kennedy, 1958-1964* (New York: W.W. Norton and Company, 1997), pp. 171, 241.

[119] Viktor Semykin, interview for, "The Missiles of October: What the World Didn't Know," *ABC News*, Journal Graphics transcript no. ABC-40, October 17, 1992, p. 21. ·

[120] Avner Cohen, *Israel and the Bomb* (New York: Columbia University Press, 1998), p. 342. Professor John Mearsheimer notes: "Egypt and Syria knew that Israel had nuclear weapons in 1973, but nevertheless they launched massive land offensives against Israel." See Mearsheimer, op. cit., p. 132.

[121] Henry Kissinger, *Year of Upheaval* (Boston: Little Brown & Co., 1982), p. 465.

decision to risk another war with Israel apparently followed from their extreme motivation to change the status quo and restore honor.[122] Their motivation to act overshadowed their caution, a dynamic that was outside Kissinger's "definition of rationality" and easy deterrence projections.

The difficult deterrence narrative is driven by the point that this variability in leadership decision-making means that *deterrence is not easy*, in part because deterrence planning must be done "with reference to the unique details of the case in hand."[123] In contemporary deterrence policy jargon, this narrative has evolved to include the corresponding point that deterrence strategies must be "tailored" to take into account the unique context and characteristics of the opponent in question.[124] The contention that doing so is critical for deterrence is hardly new. In 1962, while not using the words "tailored deterrence," Herman Kahn identified the need to understand an opponent's unique character and objectives as top requirements for deterrence planning.[125] And, in 1983, the bipartisan President's Commission on Strategic Forces (Scowcroft Commission) said in its report, "Deterrence is the set of beliefs in the minds of the Soviet leaders, given their own values and attitudes....It requires us to determine, as best we can, what would deter them

---

[122] Craig and George, op. cit., pp. 188, 191.

[123] Colin Gray, *Maintaining Effective Deterrence* (Carlisle, PA: Strategic Studies Institute, U.S. Army War College, August 2003), p. 15.

[124] Office of the Secretary of Defense, *2018 Nuclear Posture Review*, pp. 25-27. For an early post-Cold War (1996) discussion of the need to "tailor" deterrence, see Keith Payne, *Deterrence In the Second Nuclear Age*, op. cit., pp. 128-129, 156-157.

[125] Herman Kahn, "Some Comments on Controlled War," in Knorr and Read, eds., *Limited Strategic War*, op. cit., p.56.

from considering aggression, even in a crisis — not to determine what would deter us."[126]

Consequently, deterrence planning must reflect an understanding of the potentially unique values or assets held most dear by different opponents because those values or assets may vary and yet must be put at risk for deterrence purposes. The easy deterrence narrative typically contends that a punitive U.S. threat to an opponent's societal infrastructure reliably constitutes a near universally applicable deterrence threat. But, having an arsenal to threaten "easy" societal targets may be inadequate for deterrence because the material assets or intangible values opponents hold most dear may vary, i.e., they may *not be societal assets*. Consequently, this difficult deterrence narrative contends that deterrence requirements must include the nuclear capabilities needed to hold *additional or other* sets of opponents' values and assets at risk. Thus, deterrence requirements include having the nuclear forces capable of threatening a spectrum of plausible opponent values and assets, potentially including an opponent's diverse and hardened military targets. To focus on one general form of punitive deterrence threat — per the easy deterrence narrative — risks having a strategy that does not apply to the opponent in question when necessary. That risk could be extreme when the consequences of deterrence failure are extreme.

For nuclear deterrence during the Cold War, the variability in perceptions and decision-making meant recognizing that Soviet leaders, *not* American academics or officials, would "define and judge what [Soviet leaders] mean by prudence and caution."[127] As Colin Gray observed

---

[126] President's Commission on Strategic Forces, *Report of the President's Commission on Strategic Forces* (April 1983), p. 3.

[127] Herman Kahn and Keith Payne, "U.S.-Soviet Balance of Power, 1980-1990: A Decade of Confusion, Contradiction, and Complexity," in

at the time, the Soviet Union is "a culturally distinctive adversary" with unique characteristics pertinent to deterrence planning, and thus U.S. plans for deterrence must leave behind the "strategic-cultural mirror-imaging" underlying confidence that threatening Soviet society would provide reliable deterrence.[128] Correspondingly, Kahn insisted that effective U.S. nuclear deterrence required a broader nuclear threat than to societal assets: *"At the minimum, an adequate deterrent for the United States must provide an objective basis for a Soviet calculation that would persuade them that, no matter how skillful or ingenious they were, an attack on the United States would lead to a very high risk if not certainty of large-scale destruction to Soviet civil society and military forces."*[129]

Kahn fully acknowledged that his definition of an "adequate deterrent," "demands more and better offensive forces, both to destroy Soviet offensive force (if appropriate or feasible) and to threaten the Soviets so that intrawar deterrence (controlled response) is more likely to work."[130] Kahn's emphasis on the need for "more and better" nuclear forces and targeting options was not based on the simplistic notion that the larger the number of weapons the greater the deterrent effect, but that the nuclear forces needed to meet U.S. requirements for deterrence leverage against the Soviet

---

Strategic Source Book (Croton-on-Hudson, NY: Hudson Research Services, 1981), p. 3.

[128] Gray, *Nuclear Strategy and Strategic Planning*, op. cit., p. 78.

[129] Herman Kahn, *On Thermonuclear War* (Princeton, NJ: Princeton University Press, 1960), p. 557 (Emphasis in original).

[130] Herman Kahn, "United States Central War Policy," in Goldwin, ed., *Beyond the Cold War*, op. cit., p. 51. Decades following Kahn's classic work, Georgetown University Professor Matthew Kroenig's detailed analysis of case studies concludes that superiority in force numbers has indeed provided greater deterrence leverage and an exploitable advantage in contests of wills. See, Matthew Kroenig, *The Logic of American Nuclear Strategy: Why Strategic Superiority Matters* (New York: Oxford University Press, 2018).

Union demanded *more nuclear capabilities and threat options, and more credible threats* than were plausible per the easy deterrence narrative's prescribed force structure. In accord with the easy deterrence narrative, Kahn acknowledged that it would be "reckless" for an opponent to be so provocative as to risk the destruction of its society, but he added that it would be even more reckless for the United States to base its security on the easy deterrence expectation of a predictable, sensible opponent.[131]

Kahn frequently noted that deterrence might work easily, but that deterrence strategies must be established not only for occasions when deterrence can work easily, but for occasions when deterrence is much more challenging. He likened this to the need to construct buildings not just for mild weather, but for stormy weather as well. Thus, the United States must design "military and non-military systems which are sufficiently flexible to meet the complexities of the real world."[132] Indeed, the logic of the difficult deterrence narrative is captured by Kahn's observation that planning for deterrence should not be limited to expectations of "a complacent and cautious enemy. Even a frown might do that [deter]. Our attitude should be the same as an engineer's when he puts up a structure designed to last twenty years or so. He does not ask, 'Will it stand up on a pleasant June day?' He asks how it performs under stress, under hurricane, earthquake, snow load, fire, flood, thieves, fools and vandals....Deterrence is at least as important as a building, and we should have the same attitude toward our deterrent systems. We may not be able to predict the loads it will have to carry, but we are certain there will be loads of unexpected or implausible severity."[133]

---

[131] Kahn, *On Thermonuclear War*, op. cit., p. 199.

[132] Ibid., p. 190.

[133] Ibid., pp. 137-138.

The Difficult Deterrence Narrative and U.S. Policy

Recognition of the potential significance of variability for the functioning of deterrence has had considerable impact on U.S. policy development. By the mid-1970s, with policy initiatives led by Defense Secretary James Schlesinger, the official definition of the U.S. "assured destruction" deterrence metric reportedly focused less on a threat of massive societal destruction and more on graduated options and threats to disrupt Soviet internal political control and reduce Soviet military and post-war economic recovery capabilities.[134] Secretary Schlesinger observed in 1974 that deterrence required, "both more limited responses than destroying cities and advanced planning tailored to such lesser responses. Nuclear threats to our strategic forces, whether limited or large-scale, might well call for an option to respond in kind against the attacker's military forces. In other words, to be credible, and hence effective over the range of possible contingencies, deterrence must rest on many options and on a spectrum of capabilities...to support these options."[135]

By the late 1970s, there was an apparent *bipartisan U.S. consensus against* the easy deterrence notion that threats of societal destruction alone can be a reliable deterrent and McNamara's earlier "assured destruction" deterrence metric. For example, in 1978, the Carter Administration's Secretary of Defense Harold Brown observed that, "Our nuclear strategy includes not only assured destruction, but the flexibility to launch controlled counter-attacks against a

---

[134] See William Van Cleave and Roger Barnett, "Strategic Adaptability," *Orbis*, Vol. 28, No. 3 (Fall 1974), p. 666. See also, Donald Rumsfeld, *Annual Defense Department Report FY 1978* (Washington, D.C.: USGPO, January 17, 1977), p. 68.

[135] Schlesinger, *Annual Defense Department Report, FY 1975*, op. cit., p. 38.

wide range of targets."[136]   In 1979, Secretary Brown
elaborated: "It is tempting to believe, I realize, that the
threat to destroy some number of cities — along with their
population and industry — will serve as an all-purpose
deterrent. The forces required to implement such a threat
can be relatively modest....Unfortunately, however, a
[deterrence] strategy based on assured destruction alone no
longer is wholly credible....a strategy and a force structure
designed only for assured destruction is not sufficient for
our [deterrence] purposes."[137]

Instead, the Carter Administration concluded that for
deterrence purposes the United States, "must have plans for
attacks which pose a more credible threat than an all-out
attack on Soviet industry and cities. These plans should
include options to attack the targets that comprise the Soviet
military force structure needed and political power
structure, and to hold back a significant reserve." This
deterrence requirement included the U.S. capability to hold
at risk, "in a selective and measured way, a range of
military, industrial, and political control targets, while
retaining an assured destruction capacity in reserve." [138]
Consequently, the Carter Administration emphasized that
U.S. deterrence requirements included not only capabilities
for a large-scale threat to easy societal targets, but also
flexible, graduated options, and the nuclear forces needed
to threaten "a comprehensive set of targets, including
targets of political and military as well as economic
value."[139] Secretary Brown explained that these changes to
U.S. "deterrent strategy" followed from "a specific

---

[136] Harold Brown, *Department of Defense Annual Report Fiscal Year 1979*
(Washington, D.C.: USGPO, February 1978), p. 256.

[137] Harold Brown, *Department of Defense Annual Report Fiscal Year 1980*
(Washington, D.C.: USGPO, January 25, 1979), pp. 75-76.

[138] Harold Brown, *Department of Defense Annual Report Fiscal Year 1981*
(Washington, D.C.: USGPO, January 29, 1980), p. 66.

[139] Ibid., p. 6.

recognition that our strategy has to be aimed at what the Soviets think is important to them."[140]

These deterrence requirements go well beyond the earlier "easy" societal destruction metric. The apparent deterrence rationale for them was twofold: 1) because the Soviet Union possessed the capability to respond with a devastating attack against U.S. society, a U.S. deterrent threat to destroy Soviet society was deemed to be *incredible* vis-à-vis *almost any limited Soviet threat to the United States*; and, 2) because, "the things highly valued by the Soviet leadership appear to include not only lives and prosperity of the peoples of the Soviet Union, but the military, industrial and political sources of power of the regime itself."[141] That is, the Soviet leadership's highest values included its political control and military power assets, and thus the United States had to be capable of threatening these values to deter Moscow in extreme circumstances; this became a declared standard of adequacy for U.S. nuclear forces. As Secretary Brown concluded, "The unquestioned Soviet attainment of strategic parity has put the final nail in the coffin of what we long knew was dead — the notion that

---

[140] Testimony by Defense Secretary Harold Brown in, U.S. Senate, Committee on Foreign Relations, *Nuclear War Strategy*, Hearing, 96th Congress, 2nd Session, September 16, 1980 (Washington, D.C.: 1981), p. 10. (Hearing held on September 16, 1980; sanitized and printed on February 18, 1981).

[141] Harold Brown, *Department of Defense Annual Report Fiscal Year 1981*, op. cit., p. 67. Secretary Brown elaborated elsewhere on this list of most valued Soviet assets that needed to be held at risk for deterrence purposes: "Soviet leaders appear to value most — political and military control, military force both nuclear and conventional, and the industrial capability to sustain war." *Remarks Prepared For Delivery By The Honorable Harold Brown, Secretary of Defense, At The Convocation Ceremonies For The 97th Naval War College Class*, Naval War College, Newport, Rhode Island, August 20, 1980, *New Release*, Office of Assistant Secretary of Defense, Public Affairs, No. 344-80 (August 20, 1980), p. 7.

we could adequately deter the Soviets solely by threatening massive retaliation against their cities."[142]

The need to hold Soviet political and military capabilities, including nuclear, at risk for deterrence purposes also reportedly followed from the conclusion that Soviet notions of wartime victory over the West were dependent on its expansive military capabilities and its capacity for post-war economic recovery and political control.   As Colin Gray explained at the time, the "fundamental" U.S. deterrence requirement is that, "the Soviet Union would anticipate defeat in the event of war; this is a 'denial of victory' approach. Second, it is believed that victory, in Soviet terms (which are the ones that matter if the U.S. deterrent is to be a deterrent), is impossible if the essential military, paramilitary, and police assets of the state are damaged to the point where they cannot perform their functions and/or if the political control function of the Soviet state cannot operate at the minimum essential level."[143]

Correspondingly, the Carter Administration concluded that threatening Soviet military capabilities and instruments of post-war recovery constituted a deterrent threat uniquely effective to prevent Soviet attack.   The Carter Administration labeled this the Countervailing Strategy for deterrence, "designed with the Soviets in mind." As reported, it was based on a victory-denial concept of deterrence which demanded flexible nuclear threat options and was a "natural evolution of the conceptual foundations built over a generation."[144] Deterrence continued under the Reagan Administration to be based on this threat orientation and the full range of

---

[142] Harold Brown, *Department of Defense Annual Report Fiscal Year 1982* (Washington, D.C.: USGPO, January 19, 1981), p. 39.

[143] Gray, *Nuclear Strategy and Strategic Planning*, op. cit., pp. 40-41.

[144] Harold Brown, *Department of Defense Annual Report Fiscal Year 1982*, op. cit., pp. 38-42.

nuclear capabilities needed to deny the Soviet Union any plausible anticipation of gaining its political/military objectives via war.[145]

In 1983, the bipartisan President's Commission on Strategic Forces (Scowcroft Commission) confirmed and elaborated on these deterrence strategy developments of the earlier Carter Administration: "Our strategic forces must be modernized, as necessary, to enhance to an adequate degree their overall survivability and to enable them to engage effectively the targets that Soviet leaders most value." And,

> In order to deter such Soviet [nuclear] threats we must be able to put at risk those types of Soviet targets—including hardened ones such as military command bunkers and facilities, missile silos, nuclear weapons and other storage, and the rest— which the Soviet leaders have given every indication by their actions they value most, and which constitute their tools of control and power. We cannot afford the delusion that Soviet leaders— human though they are and cautious though we hope they will be—are going to be deterred by exactly the same concerns that would dissuade us.[146]

In 1986, Caspar Weinberger, the Reagan Administration's Secretary of Defense, even stated publicly that U.S. deterrence planning did *not* seek, "to maximize Soviet casualties or to attack deliberately the Soviet population.

---

[145] Caspar Weinberger, *Annual Report to the Congress, Fiscal Year 1984* (Washington, D.C.: USGPO, February 1, 1983), pp. 32, 51, 57. See also, The White House, *Nuclear Weapons Employment Policy, National Security Decision Directive Number 13*, pp. 1-2. (Declassified May 1, 2017). Available at the National Security Archive, George Washington University, nsarchive@gwu.edu.

[146] President's Commission on Strategic Forces, *Report of the President's Commission on Strategic Forces*, op. cit., p. 6.

Indeed, we believe such a doctrine would be neither moral nor prudent." Instead, "secure deterrence should be based on the threat to destroy what the Soviet leadership values most highly: Namely, itself, its military power and political control capabilities, and its industrial ability to wage war."[147] This suggested a near-complete repudiation of the easy deterrence narrative and Secretary McNamara's earlier characterization of an "assured destruction"-oriented deterrent.

Many proponents of the easy deterrence narrative understandably responded quite negatively to these U.S. deterrence policy initiatives under Republican and Democratic presidents. These bipartisan policy developments moved U.S. policy well beyond the easy deterrence narrative's modest and narrowly-defined boundaries for "stable" nuclear deterrence capabilities; *instead they advanced as a deterrence requirement U.S. nuclear forces disdained by that narrative.* The priority U.S. goal remained deterrence, but the official declared approach to deterrence shifted from the relatively modest and narrow nuclear second-strike capabilities needed to threaten societal assets to a deterrence metric that included limited nuclear options and the flexibility to threaten a comprehensive range of Soviet targets.

The differences separating these easy and difficult deterrence narratives are so stark that proponents of the former often contend that the latter is not a deterrence strategy whatsoever and instead is for nuclear "war-fighting." One well-known proponent of the easy deterrence narrative labeled these bipartisan policy developments, "flexible madness." [148] Another lamented that, "Deterrence once meant reluctance to attack for fear of

---

[147] Caspar Weinberger, "U.S. Defense Strategy," *Foreign Affairs*, Vol. 64, No. 4 (Spring 1986), p. 682.

[148] See for example, Herbert Scoville, "Flexible Madness?," *Foreign Policy*, Vol. XIV (Spring 1974), pp. 164-177.

being unacceptably damaged. [An] assured 'second strike' capability—200 protected weapons—was considered an adequate deterrent. But military tradition and nationalist competition require superiority and winning, not deterring....ignoring overkill limits."[149] The diverse nuclear capabilities and flexibility identified by Republican and Democratic administrations as necessary for deterrence — as prescribed by the difficult deterrence narrative—were deemed unnecessary and/or "destabilizing" and as being designed for "war-fighting" purposes, *not* deterrence. They have continued to be so criticized to the present.[150]

However, the difficult deterrence narrative's call for the flexibility of nuclear capabilities needed to threaten a spectrum of opponents' assets, including hardened military

---

[149] Seymour Melman, "Limits of Military Power," *The New York Times*, October 17, 1980.

[150] See for example Andrew Facini, "The Low-Yield Nuclear Warhead: A Dangerous Weapon Based on Bad Strategic Thinking," *Bulletin of the Atomic Scientists*, January 28, 2020, available at https://thebulletin.org/2020/01/the-low-yield-nuclear-warhead-a-dangerous-weapon-based-on-bad-strategic-thinking/?utm_source=Members&utm_campaign=700d6e5657-EMAIL_CAMPAIGN_2020_01_28_04_20&utm_medium=email&utm_te rm=0_e842221dc2-700d6e5657-147762833. See also Thomas Nichols, professor at the U.S. Naval War College, readily acknowledges that the type of force posture typically associated with the easy deterrence narrative is "inflexible" and "...forecloses the ability to engage in iterated rounds of strikes that might offer the hope of 'intrawar' deterrence, in which gradual escalation to greater destruction helps to put a stop to the conflict before it reaches all-out nuclear war." *No Use: Nuclear Weapons and U.S. National Security*, op. cit., p. 97; see also pp. 102-109. See also, Thomas Nichols, "Time to Change America's Atomic Arsenal," *The Diplomat*, March, 2013, available at http://thediplomat.com/2013/03/time-to-change-americas-atomic-arsenal/; and Hans Kristensen and Robert Norris, *Reviewing Nuclear Guidance: Putting Obama's Words Into Action*, Arms Control Association, November 2, 2011, available at http://www.armscontrol.org/act/2011_11/Reviewing_Nuclear_Guidance_Putting_Obama_Words_Into_Action.

targets, and to adapt ("tailor") U.S. deterrence strategies to the potentially unique values and perceptions of opponents *presents a different approach to deterrence. It may be criticized as such, but its goal is deterrence.* As Gray observes, the charge that diverse capabilities and flexibility are inconsistent with deterrence simply does "not understand that societal punishment is only one approach to deterrence, that it is not synonymous with deterrence."[151]

The call for diversity and flexibility in U.S. nuclear policy has endured and advanced. For example, in 2013, the Obama Administration's unclassified nuclear employment strategy emphasized publicly that its deterrence policy would not follow the easy deterrence narrative. Rather, it would maintain, "significant counterforce [i.e., counter-military] capabilities," and "does not rely on a 'counter-value' [i.e., counter-societal] or 'minimum deterrence' strategy." It would instead "seek to minimize collateral damage to civilian populations and civilian objects. The United States will not intentionally target civilian populations or civilian objects."[152]

In 2016, Obama Administration Assistant Secretary of Defense Robert Scher testified before Congress that for deterrence the United States requires "credible proportionate response options."[153] The same year, ADM

---

[151] Gray, *Nuclear Strategy and Strategic Planning*, op. cit., p. 29.

[152] Department of Defense, *Report on Nuclear Employment Strategy of the United States Specified in Section 491 of 10 U.S.C.*, June 2013, pp. 4-5, at https://www.globalsecurity.org/wmd/library/dod/us-nuclear-employment-strategy.pdf.

[153] Robert Scher, "Statement of Robert Scher, Assistant Secretary of Defense for Strategy, Plans and Capabilities," 114th U.S. Congress, House Armed Services Committee, March 2, 2016, p. 5, available at https://docs.house.gov/meetings/AS/AS29/20160302/104619/HHRG-114-AS29-Wstate-ScherR-20160302.pdf. Similarly, in 2016, former Obama Administration Defense Secretary Leon Panetta observed that deterrence credibility demands that the United States be able to respond to a nuclear attack "in kind." Quoted in Brian Everstine, "Thornberry: Expect Nuclear Tests During the Lame Duck," *Air Force Magazine*,

Cecil Haney, the Commander of U.S. Strategic Command, said, "We must ensure that we have a credible strategic nuclear deterrent that has diversity and flexibility such that no adversaries can think that they will benefit from escalating to include the employment of a nuclear weapon, that it will be costly to them, and that restraint is a better option."[154]

Brad Roberts, the Obama Administration's Deputy Assistant Secretary of Defense with responsibility for nuclear policy, explains the Obama Administration's view of U.S. deterrence requirements and its corresponding plan for the comprehensive modernization of America's aging nuclear systems. The administration apparently rejected the easy deterrence narrative as the basis for policy because it would preclude the flexibility needed for credible graduated deterrence threats and the capacity to "tailor" U.S. deterrence strategies to the unique character of opponents and the emerging strategic context—including the capabilities particularly important to deter opponents' "theories of victory."[155] Such an approach to deterrence was consistent with earlier Democratic and Republican administrations and the difficult deterrence narrative.

Obama Administration calls to rebuild U.S. strategic nuclear forces, after decades of relative inactivity,[156] appear

---

December 2, 2016, available at http://www.airforcemag.com/DRArchive/Pages/2016/December%20 2016/December%2002%202016/Thornberry-Expect-Nuclear-Tests-During-the-Lame-Duck.aspx.

[154] Cecil D. Haney, "An Interview with Cecil D. Haney," *Joint Forces Quarterly*, Vol. 83, 4th Quarter (2016), p. 68.

[155] Brad Roberts, *The Case for U.S. Nuclear Weapons in The 21st Century* (Stanford, CA: Stanford University Press, 2016), pp. 35, 99, 103-104, 192-194, 260-262, 268-271.

[156] As described by Defense Secretary Ashton Carter in, Secretary of Defense Ash Carter, "Remarks by Secretary Carter to Troops at Minot Air Force Base, North Dakota," September 26, 2016, available at https://www.defense.gov/Newsroom/Transcripts/Transcript/Article

to reflect basic themes of the difficult deterrence narrative and, correspondingly, the need for U.S. nuclear modernization.   Indeed, opponents of this rebuilding program, largely following the easy deterrence narrative, criticized the Obama Administration sharply for having "lost focus and momentum" and for pursuing "excessive strategic capabilities."[157] They complained that "it is past time for the Obama administration to take a hard look at where the U.S. nuclear arsenal is heading....It is time to change course."[158]

Nevertheless, the Obama Administration sustained its nuclear modernization plans.   The same underlying difficult deterrence themes appear in the 2018 *Nuclear Posture Review* and are apparent in the Trump Administration's continuation of the nuclear rebuilding programs.   As Admiral Richard observed, "Our nuclear forces must include a sufficient range of capabilities such that Russia never mistakenly perceives any advantage from using nuclear weapons, at any threshold of violence," and, pointing to the need for "tailored" deterrence strategies, "it's the inherent flexibility in the triad that enables me to execute those strategies."[159]

/956079/remarks-by-secretary-carter-to-troops-at-minot-air-force-base-north-dakota/.

[157] Daryl Kimball, "Mr. President, 'Yes, We Can,'" *Arms Control Today*, ArmsControl.org, July 8, 2015, available at http://www.armscontrol.org/ACT/2015_0708/Focus/Mr-President-Yes-We-Can.

[158] Tom Collina, Will Saetren, "Time to Cut America's Nuclear Triad," *The National Interest*, December 17, 2015, available at http://nationalinterest.org/feature/time-cut-americas-nuclear-triad-14650?page=show.

[159] See, Admiral Charles Richard, *Statement of Charles A. Richard, Commander of United States Strategic Command Before the Senate Committee on Armed Services*, February 13, 2020, pp. 5-6; and, C. Todd Lopez, "Stratcom Commander: Failing to Replace Nuclear Triad Akin to Disarmament," *DoD News*, February 28, 2020.

The Difficult Deterrence Narrative and Physically Defending Against Nuclear Attack

The differences separating the easy and difficult deterrence narratives go beyond the latter's greater requirements for strategic nuclear capabilities. For *a select cadre of those contributing to* the difficult deterrence narrative, including Herman Kahn, Donald Brennan, and Colin Gray, it also included the requirement for capabilities to physically defend the United States from nuclear attack. Their contention regarding the deterrence requirement for strategic defensive capabilities follows again from the potential significance for deterrence of the variation in leadership decision-making — in this case revolving around *the need for deterrence threat credibility.*

In some cases, uncertainty or chance attending a deterrence threat may be adequate for deterrence to function predictably — as expected by the easy narrative. In other cases, however, much greater threat credibility may be needed: to be deterred, the opponent may need to perceive *more than a "chance"* that its aggression would lead to great cost.[160] Such a chance by definition means that the opponent also perceives a "chance" that its provocation *will not lead to great cost* — an opportunity that some risk-tolerant/highly-motivated opponents might choose to exploit. That is, the "chance" of no severe U.S. response might actually motivate some opponents to move provocatively as opposed to standing back from their desired provocative course. Correspondingly, the difficult deterrence narrative contends that in some cases a *more*

---

[160] Lawrence Freedman looks at the significance of credibility to the functioning of deterrence and draws from the analysis of domestic crime as an analogy: "Changing the marginal severity of punishments therefore appears to have far less [deterrent] effect than *increasing the certainty* that crime will result in some punishment." Lawrence Freedman, *Deterrence*, op. cit., p. 64. (Emphasis added).

credible threat may be essential to the effectiveness of deterrence and require additional capabilities or actions to convey that credibility.

Herman Kahn was particularly critical of the contention that uncertainty or chance can provide sufficient threat credibility for reliable deterrence.   He contended that opponents may perceive a deterrence threat based on chance as a bluff—not as an effective deterrent to opponents willing to take risks.[161]   Indeed, he referred to the modest force requirements that follow from the easy deterrence narrative as providing only a deterrence "façade."[162]

Kahn emphasized the connection between physically defending the United States and having a *sufficiently credible* extended nuclear deterrent for allies. He insisted that: 1) a "not incredible" U.S. deterrence threat is needed to extend deterrence coverage to allies; and, 2) achieving *that level of threat credibility is dependent on the U.S. capability to protect American society to some extent.*[163] Consequently, for Kahn, an adequate U.S. extended deterrent requires U.S. capabilities that are disdained by the easy deterrence narrative, i.e., some capabilities to physically protect U.S. society from nuclear attack.   Why so?   Because for an opponent to believe that the United States might execute its deterrence threat on behalf of an ally, the opponent must believe that the United States, "might conceivably prefer to go to war rather than acquiesce on some vital interest."[164]

---

[161] Kahn, "United States Central War Policy," in Goldwin, ed., *Beyond the Cold War*, op. cit., p. 51.

[162] Ibid., p. 46.

[163] Kahn's argument linking the needed credibility of extended deterrence to a measure of U.S. societal defense continues to the present. See Jina Kim and John K. Warden, "Limiting North Korea's Coercive Nuclear Leverage," *Survival*, 62:1, p. 36, DOI: 10.1080/00396338.2020.1715062, available at https://doi.org/10.1080/00396338.2020.1715062.

[164] Kahn, "Some Comments on Controlled War," in Knorr and Read, eds., *Limited Strategic War*, op. cit., p. 61.

Kahn argued that in a true "balance of terror," the U.S. extended deterrent was unlikely to be credible because the opponent's nuclear threat to the United States could be seen as precluding U.S. willingness to employ nuclear weapons on behalf of an ally — such an act could, in effect, be suicidal and thus not adequately credible for deterrence. His basic point was that deterrence credibility is based not only on the U.S. threat that can be posed against an opponent, but on the punishment the opponent would inflict in return on the United States if Washington were to carry out its deterrent threat. If an opponent's punishment of the United States is likely to be intolerable, even if the U.S. deterrent threat is recognized as severe by the opponent, *that threat may not be sufficiently credible to deter in a crisis* because the opponent will likely see it as a bluff to be called: "Credibility depends on being willing to accept the other side's retaliatory blow. It depends on the harm *he* can do, not [only] on the harm we can do."[165]

In short, according to Kahn, if U.S. society is fully vulnerable to an opponent's nuclear capability, i.e., if U.S. society is wholly undefended against nuclear attack, the United States cannot credibly threaten that opponent with nuclear weapons on behalf of an ally because doing so could be an irrational, self-destructive act for the United States. A sufficiently *credible* U.S. nuclear deterrence threat for allies *must not* be based on a threatened U.S. action that would likely result in the opponent's subsequent destruction of the United States — such a threat is illogical: "It will be irrational [for the United States] to attack and thus insure a Soviet retaliation unless we have made preparations to counter this retaliation."[166]

Kahn was hardly alone in making the connection between the credibility of deterrence and capabilities for

---

[165] Kahn, *On Thermonuclear War*, op. cit., p. 32. (Emphasis in original).
[166] Ibid., p. 133.

strategic defense. In 1979, Sir Michael Howard observed that, "Peoples who are not prepared to make the effort necessary for operational defense are even less likely to support a decision to initiate a nuclear exchange from which they will themselves suffer almost inconceivable destruction."[167]

According to Kahn's corresponding line of thought here, a sufficiently *credible* U.S. extended deterrence threat requires U.S. defenses against an opponent's nuclear forces to limit the risk of damage to American society that the United States must run in its extension of nuclear deterrence to allies. In effect, Kahn contends that credible extended deterrence demands that the risks run by extending deterrence must not manifestly outweigh the value being protected or opponents may see that extended deterrent as a bluff—thus the logical need to physically defend U.S. society to provide the necessary condition for *credible* extended deterrence. Gray concurred with Kahn's basic point during the Cold War, concluding that "the deterrence case for homeland" defense is persuasive because the credibility of U.S. extended deterrence "is very low so long as the United States makes no noteworthy provision for the protection of its homeland against inevitable Soviet retaliation."[168] There certainly is some historical evidence that countries with nuclear capabilities to threaten the United States homeland will feel at greater liberty to challenge the United States regionally. Indeed, during the Cold War, Soviet doctrine included the point that Soviet achievement of such nuclear capabilities gave the Soviet Union greater freedom to confront the United States

---

[167] Michael Howard, "The Forgotten Dimensions of Strategy," *Foreign Affairs*, Vol. 57, No. 5 (Summer 1979), p. 983.

[168] Gray, *Nuclear Strategy and Strategic Planning*, op. cit., pp. 82-83.

regionally because it degraded the credibility of U.S. extended nuclear deterrence threats.[169]

The types of strategic capabilities that could help make U.S. extended deterrence guarantees credible in this way are varied. They could include offensive systems able to destroy the opponent's nuclear strike forces on the ground prior to their launch, defensive systems designed to destroy the opponent's nuclear strike forces after launch and while they are enroute to the United States, and passive defenses intended to shelter or otherwise protect U.S. society. Neither Kahn nor Gray suggest that for deterrence purposes such defenses must be "perfect" (likely a hopeless goal), but rather sufficiently effective to lead the opponent to conclude that it cannot dismiss the U.S. extended nuclear deterrent given its own nuclear capabilities. The corresponding variant of the difficult deterrence narrative contends that U.S. extended deterrence responsibilities establish this requirement for some U.S. homeland defensive capabilities that the easy deterrence narrative deems uniquely "destabilizing."

Another separate but related rationale for strategic defense capabilities follows logically from the theme that deterrence is difficult to establish and maintain, and subject to potential failure. Kahn emphasized that because deterrence can fail despite best efforts to deter, the United States requires some defensive capabilities to reduce the level of possible catastrophe in the event of war. This is a matter of national prudence. As Kahn noted, his approach to deterrence is, "much more preoccupied...with the possibility that war can happen and with the necessity for being able to alleviate the consequences of war if it

---

[169] For a discussion of this point of Soviet doctrine, see Keith B. Payne, *Nuclear Deterrence in U.S.-Soviet Relations* (Boulder, CO: Westview Press, 1981), pp. 85-97, 110-113.

occurs,"[170] and, "War can still occur and it is better to survive the war than not. Therefore one needs to have systems that can reduce the damage done in a war."[171] He emphasized that, "so long as" strategic defensive capabilities are "technologically and economically possible," they are needed for both deterrence purposes and "because it is prudent to take out insurance against a war's occurring unintentionally."[172] Kahn's colleague, Donald Brennan, elaborated the case for strategic defense of the United States during the Cold War, arguing that it was "bizarre" that U.S. policy should prioritize offensive threats to Russians over defensive capabilities for Americans.[173]

In short, a variant of the difficult deterrence narrative emphasizes the requirement for some physical defense of society, both to provide deterrence credibility and — because "war can happen" — to defend American society to the extent feasible. This call for defensive capabilities for the sake of societal protection obviously contrasts sharply with the easy deterrence narrative's rejection of societal defensive capabilities as unnecessary and "destabilizing," as well as generally infeasible and unaffordable. Pointing to this requirement reflects a different understanding of the conditions needed for deterrence stability and a comparably

---

[170] Kahn, "United States Central War Policy," in Goldwin, ed., *Beyond the Cold War*, op. cit., p. 51.

[171] Kahn, "Some Comments on Controlled War," in Knorr and Read, eds., *Limited Strategic War*, op. cit., p. 64.

[172] Kahn, *The Nature and Feasibility of War and Deterrence*, op. cit., pp. 39-40. Colin Gray presented this point concisely: "Nuclear war is possible, and the U.S. government owes it to generations of Americans — past, present, and future — to make prudent defense preparations to limit damage to domestic American values to the extent feasible in the event of nuclear war." Gray, *Nuclear Strategy and Strategic Planning*, op. cit., p. 8.

[173] Donald G. Brennan, "The Case for Population Defense," in Johan Holst and William Schneider, eds., *Why ABM: Policy Issues in the Missile Defense Controversy* (New York: Pergamon Press, 1969), p. 116.

different understanding of the value of physical defenses for the United States.

Kahn, Brennan and Gray were mindful of the technical and financial challenges confronting these strategic defense goals, but contended that the level of defenses needed for extended deterrence *credibility* was likely available, and that a meaningful level of strategic defense for society could be available with reasonable investment, time and policy attention. Indeed, some strategic defense proponents contended that the primary impediment to U.S. policy acceptance was the presumption against strategic defense established by the easy deterrence narrative rather than any insuperable technical or cost challenges: "Strategic defenses were rejected not on strategic grounds but because they did not conform to the theories of mutual deterrence and arms control which themselves have proved invalid."[174]

It should be noted that some scholars who fully rejected the easy deterrent narrative had little confidence in the potential for the physical defense of U.S. society against Soviet nuclear attack. Instead, they advocated for U.S. nuclear escalation options to deter Soviet escalation and thereby reduce potential damage to the United States.[175]

U.S. Policy Regarding Physical Defenses Against Strategic Attack

U.S. policy has moved incrementally and on a bipartisan basis over the past several decades towards acceptance of strategic ballistic missile defense capabilities for the United States *against limited* missile threats and theater missile

---

[174] Benson Adams, "In Defense of the Homeland," *U.S. Naval Proceedings*, Vol. 109, No. 6 (June 1983), p. 49.

[175] See the discussion in William R. Van Cleave, "The US Strategic Triad," in *The US War Machine*, Ray Bonds, ed. (New York: Crown Publishers, Inc., 1983), pp. 67-68.

defenses for allies and friends.[176]   This move in policy toward defensive capabilities for the United States against limited missile threats appears to have been motivated by the emerging and unprecedented nuclear threats from "rogue" states: "In such a world, Cold War deterrence is no longer enough to maintain peace, to protect our own citizens and our own allies and friends....We need a new framework that allows us to build missile defenses to counter the different threats of today's world."[177] Gen. John Hyten, Vice Chairman of the Joint Chiefs of Staff, identifies the North Korean missile threat to the United States as the reason behind U.S. strategic missile defenses: "That's what they are built for. They're built for North Korea. They're not built for anything else..."[178] This goal corresponds to an apparent general view that U.S. missile defense capabilities are technically feasible/affordable against a *limited* strategic missile threat—as opposed to the contemporary prospects

---

[176] Department of Defense, Office of the Secretary of Defense, *2019 Missile Defense Review* (January 19, 2019), pp. 25-37. The Obama Administration's 2010 *Ballistic Missile Defense Review* lists as first priority defending "the homeland against the threat of limited ballistic missile attack." Department of Defense, Office of Public Affairs, *2010 Ballistic Missile Defense Review (BMDR) Fact Sheet*, March 3, 2010, p. 2.

[177] See, President George W. Bush, *Text of President Bush's Speech at the National Defense University*, May 1, 2002, *The New York Times on the Web*, Associated Press, available at http://www.nytimes.com/aponline/national/01WIRE-BUSH-TEXT.html?pagewanted+print. See also, Department of Defense, *Nuclear Posture Review: Report to the Congress in Response to Sections 1041 (as Amended) and 1042 of the Floyd D. Spence National Defense Authorization Act for Fiscal Year 2001, PL 106-398*, December 2001, pp. iii, 7. (Declassified).

[178] Lee Haye-ah, "U.S. Military Leader Expresses Full Confidence in Ability to Defend Against New North Korean Missiles," *Yonhap News Agency*, January 18, 2020, available at https://en.yna.co.kr/view/AEN20200118000400325.

for defending against the large-scale missile threats posed by Russia and China.[179]

A 2016 Joint Chiefs of Staff open report, *The Joint Force in a Contested and Disordered World*, underscores "the enduring requirement…to physically defend U.S. sovereign territory and citizenry against a wide range of foreign military operations," and emphasizes that "the United States will confront an increasing number of state and non-state actors with the will and capabilities to threaten targets within the homeland and U.S. citizens with the ultimate intention to coerce."[180]

---

[179] Numerous U.S. government statements observe that U.S. strategic missile defense capabilities are effective against the prospect of limited missile attacks against the United States: Gen. Hyten said most recently, "I don't say 100 percent very often. I have 100 percent confidence in those capabilities [U.S. missile defense] against North Korea." Ibid.; "The United States is currently protected against limited ICBM attacks." Department of Defense, Office of Public Affairs, *2010 BMDR Fact Sheet*, op. cit., p. 2. See also, Department of Defense, Office of the Secretary of Defense, *2019 Missile Defense Review*, op. cit., p. XII; the statement by ADM Harry Harris in, Missy Ryan, "North Korean Threat Could Require New Missile Defenses for Western U.S.," *Washington Post*, February 14, 2018, available at https://www.washingtonpost.com/world/national-security/north-korean-threat-could-require-new-missile-defenses-for-western-us/2018/02/14/80f4ba26-119a-11e8-8eal-cld91fcec3fe_story.html?utm_term=.62b5b973a913; and, the statement by Lt. Gen. Obering in, Rowen Scarborough, "U.S. Puts Faith In Missile Defense," *Washington Times*, June 24 2006, p. 1. See also, J.D. Crouch and Robert Joseph, "Tough Calls, Good Calls," *The Wall Street Journal*, January 22, 2008, p. A-19. As early as 1991, the Arms Control Association (frequently critical of missile defense) observed, "[T]here is little doubt that it is technically possible to protect the United States against a handful of missiles launched by accident, a mad commander, or a Third World country." The Arms Control Association, Background Paper, *New Star Wars Plan: Unnecessary Destruction of the ABM Treaty*, February 1991, p. 1.

[180] Joint Chiefs of Staff, *Joint Operating Environment 2035, The Joint Force in a Contested and Disordered World*, July 14, 2016, p. 24.

However, the acceptance of the need for physical protection of the United States remains within some familiar limits.   The Obama Administration's 2013 unclassified *Nuclear Employment Strategy* states explicitly that, "the United States seeks to improve strategic stability by demonstrating that it is not our intent to negate Russia's strategic nuclear deterrent."[181]   The Trump Administration's 2019 *Missile Defense Review* states: "The United States *relies on nuclear deterrence* to prevent potential Russian or Chinese nuclear attacks employing their large and technically sophisticated intercontinental missile systems."[182]   U.S. security against the large-scale nuclear threats posed by these great powers appears to be based *on continuing confidence in mutual deterrence, not* on capabilities for physical protection against such a nuclear attack.

Contending Approaches to Deterrence: Shared Starting Points, but Different Expectations, and Competing Prescriptions

As noted, both the easy and difficult deterrence narratives begin with Realist "bedrock assumptions":   the international system is anarchic; there is an inherent level of mistrust among states in the system; and, countries generally will prioritize their survival and engage in rational decision-making and behavior for this purpose.[183] They thus agree on the importance of nuclear deterrence for the United States and allies in contemporary international relations. Beyond these points of agreement, however, the easy and difficult deterrence narratives differ sharply in

---

[181] Department of Defense, *Report on Nuclear Employment Strategy of the United States Specified in Section 491 of 10 U.S.C.*, June 2013, p. 3.

[182] Department of Defense, Office of the Secretary of Defense, *2019 Missile Defense Review*, op. cit., p. 8. (Emphasis added).

[183] Mearsheimer, *The Tragedy of Great Power Politics*, pp. 30-31.

their *expectations of opponents' likely decision-making and behavior.*

These differing "extra-Realist" expectations may seem to be of academic interest only, but they drive the competing easy and difficult deterrence narratives to contradictory positions regarding the functioning of deterrence and to correspondingly contradictory conclusions regarding the requirements for deterrence. They establish different definitions of: "how much is enough?;" the types of capabilities that are consistent with deterrence "stability;" what must be done to support deterrence planning; the value of threat credibility; and, the prospective value of physically defending the United States in the event deterrence fails. These differences are the basis for *the strikingly different approaches to deterrence that have been at the heart of the U.S. deterrence policy debate from the 1960s to present-day debates about the nuclear force programs of the Obama and Trump Administrations.* The fundamental differences in their respective starting points can be summarized concisely.

The easy deterrence narrative posits a particular type of opponent (i.e., one that is predictably deterrable) in its elaboration of deterrence and thereby has considerable confidence that it has captured a reliable formula for effective deterrence. The context is a balance of terror and opponents are expected to be deterred reliably by a severe societal threat. Such a threat is relatively easy to achieve and can be sufficient to deter highly provocative attacks even if the opponent sees only a "chance" that the United States would execute its deterrent threat—vice a highly credible threat. In opponents' calculations of costs and benefits, the "crystal ball effect" unique to nuclear weapons is expected to overshadow other possible factors that might otherwise lead opponents to incaution or inattention, including their particular character, goals, history, political system, culture, values, etc.

This context and expected type of opponent lead to specific guidelines for the type and size of nuclear arsenal consistent with this deterrence narrative, i.e., the relatively modest and narrow nuclear arsenal needed to pose a societal-based second-strike threat—with some graduated options for signaling purposes.   Forces beyond that standard are unnecessary "overkill" and potentially destabilizing. Strategic defenses intended to protect society also are unnecessary for deterrence and likely destabilizing because they could upset an otherwise easily established balance of terror, *without* the potential of providing meaningful protection.

The easy deterrence narrative provides this general formula for categorizing forces as stabilizing or destabilizing. This is a significant distinction because it presents a potential avenue for arms control agreements to contribute greatly to deterrence—if they advance stabilizing forces and restrict or preclude destabilizing forces, as stability and instability are defined by this deterrence narrative.

Perhaps most characteristic of commentary informed by the easy deterrence narrative are confident and virtually universal claims about what forces will or will not be "stabilizing," and that relatively modest nuclear capabilities will provide deterrence *reliably*, harkening back to McNamara's claims about the venerable "assured destruction" construct. Also frequent are equally confident claims that force elements beyond the easy adequacy standard are *unnecessary* for deterrence, or worse, destabilizing.   Some critics of deterrence deem this confidence in deterrence to be contrary to Realist thought, and instead the product of "nuclear romantics," akin to "gentle pot-smoking dreamers."[184]

---

[184] Ward Wilson, "How Nuclear Realists Falsely Frame the Nuclear Weapons Debate," *Bulletin of the Atomic Scientists*, May 7, 2015, available

Such a criticism is understandable, if overstated. But, to adopt Kahn's construction metaphor and deterrence standards, the easy deterrence narrative's expectation of consistently "sensible" opponents who are deterred reliably by uncertain punitive threats to society is *to prepare deterrence only for fair weather*. Why so? Because there is great potential variability in opponents' calculations, there can be *no confidence* that *all* rational opponents will be uniformly cautious and prudent when they confront uncertain deterrent *threats of societal destruction*. *All* sensible opponents may not be deterred by threats perceived as having only a "chance" of being executed. Some opponents may be deterred only by *highly credible threats to much more challenging and plentiful sets of targets*. U.S. deterrence strategies must be effective against these opponents too. And even such expanded deterrence threats delivered credibly *may not deter on occasion*.

This expectation of the potential for great variability in decision-making to shape opponent responses to deterrence threats leads to considerably different requirements for deterrence than those identified by the easy deterrence narrative. Most fundamentally, it logically mandates more expansive underlying nuclear deterrent capabilities that enable the United States to hold at risk a wide range of possible targets, potentially including threatening targets as needed to pose a "victory-denial" threat to opponents. In addition, the prospective need for deterrence strategies that are *sufficiently credible* to deter even highly determined and cost tolerant opponents suggests the need for flexible, graduated and proportional threat options. This may be particularly important vis-à-vis opponents who appear to place confidence in their ability to coerce the United States via their own limited nuclear threats — as appears to be the

---

at http://thebulletin.org/2015/05/how-nuclear-realists-falsely-frame-the-nuclear-weapons-debate/.

case with contemporary Russian thinking.[185]   Per the difficult deterrence narrative, corresponding U.S. "countervailing" (using the apt label from the Carter Administration) threat capabilities may be needed to help facilitate intrawar deterrence and limits on escalation.

The difficult deterrence narrative's expectation of great potential variability in opponent decision-making also logically leads to the need to work hard to understand the unique worldviews and calculations of diverse opponents, and to tailor U.S. deterrence efforts accordingly.   The emergence of multiple opponents in the post-Cold War era likely makes this deterrence task more challenging and magnifies the importance of having this flexibility of deterrent threat.[186]   As Lawrence Freedman observes, deterrence "works best" when antagonists share norms and "a sense of appropriate behavior."[187]   But, it must also function when there is a lack of familiarity and norms are not shared. This again suggests the need for the underlying intelligence and diverse deterrent capabilities that enable

---

[185] See for example, the remarks by then-Defense Secretary Ashton Carter in, "Pentagon Chief: Russia, N. Korea Most Likely to Use 'Smaller' Scale Nuke Attacks," in Kristin Wong, *The Hill*, September 26, 2016, available at https://thehill.com/policy/defense/297892-pentagon-chief-says-next-nuclear-attack-most-likely-by-russia-or-north-korea. See also, 2018 *Nuclear Posture Review*, op. cit., pp. 8-9, 30-31; Carter, "Remarks by Secretary Carter to Troops at Minot Air Force Base, North Dakota," op. cit.; Roberts, *The Case for U.S. Nuclear Weapons In the 21st Century*, op. cit., pp. 130-138; Scher, op. cit., p. 3; and, Katarzyna Zysk, "Escalation and Nuclear Weapons in Russia's Military Strategy," *The RUSI Journal* (May 25, 2018), available at https://doi.org/10.1080/03071847.2018.1469267.

[186] As discussed in, Donald Rumsfeld, Secretary of Defense, *Annual Report to the President and the Congress, 2002*, pp. 83-84, available at https://history.defense.gov/Portals/70/Documents/annual_reports/2 002_DoD_AR.pdf?ver=2014-06-24-153732-117. See also Payne, *The Great American Gamble*, op. cit., pp. 396-398.

[187] Freedman, *Deterrence*, op. cit. p. 5.

the United States to knowingly hold at risk a wide range of potential targets for deterrence purposes.

Finally, in sharp contrast to the easy deterrence narrative, the potential variability in opponents' decision-making leads a variant of the difficult deterrence narrative to conclude that the United States must seek a level of strategic defensive capability to provide *the credibility* of threat that may be needed for extended deterrence and also to limit damage to the extent feasible in the event deterrence fails. The latter goal may be considered increasingly important with the emergence of new limited nuclear threats from non-peer opponents whose decision-making may be particularly opaque and/or eccentric.

Just as some easy deterrence proponents mistakenly charge that the difficult deterrence emphasis on threat credibility, flexibility, and diversity reflects not deterrence, but a nuclear "war-fighting" goal, critics of U.S. missile defense—arguing largely from the easy deterrence narrative—often charge that missile defense proponents are focused on war-fighting, *not* on deterrence.[188] This charge is an extension of the common but mistaken critique, noted above, that the difficult deterrence narrative *rejects* deterrence as the paramount goal in favor of nuclear "war-fighting." It mischaracterizes the points actually presented by Kahn and others, i.e., that some level of societal defenses *is critical for credible deterrence*, particularly extended deterrence, and because deterrence can fail, some defense is

---

[188] As one contemporary commentator puts it, those favoring missile defense are "those who believe the United States should possess the ability to win a nuclear war" in contrast to "those who prioritize the stability of mutual deterrence." Richard Purcell, "Nuclear Damage Limitation in an Era of Great Power Competition," *Global Security Review*, January 23, 2020, available at https://globalsecurityreview.com/nuclear-damage-limitation-great-power-competition/.

needed "to alleviate the consequences of war if it occurs";[189] or, as President Reagan suggested in 1983, "Wouldn't it be better to save lives than to avenge them?"[190] These goals *are explicitly in support of credible deterrence* and mitigating the consequences of deterrence failure to the extent possible. There is a considerable distance, conceptually and materially, between these points in favor of some defenses and the goal of and planning for "winning" a nuclear war.

There certainly is room to debate Kahn's contention that some societal defenses are necessary for extended deterrence, and whether any meaningful level of societal defense is feasible or affordable. But it is a mistake to characterize the difficult deterrence narrative's alternative approach to deterrence and missile defense *as the rejection* of deterrence in favor of "war-fighting."

Figure 2 below presents a simplified summary of the fundamental differences distinguishing the easy and difficult deterrence narratives and implications of each for U.S. deterrence requirements. It bears repeating that the narratives summarized in Figure 2 are simplified conceptual constructs that incorporate select points from the works of the preeminent scholars cited repeatedly in these pages, but do not reflect the variation, subtlety and nuance of those works.

---

[189] Kahn, "United States Central War Policy," in Goldwin, ed., *Beyond the Cold War*, op cit., p. 51.

[190] President Ronald Reagan, *Address to the Nation on Defense and National Security*, March 23, 1983, available at http://www.reagan.utexas.edu/archives/ speeches/1983/32383d.htm.

Figure 2. A Simplified Summary of Competing Deterrence Narratives[191]

Easy Deterrence	Difficult Deterrence
<u>Goal</u>. U.S. and allied security via deterrence and, if deterrence initially fails, the prevention of escalation by the re-establishment of deterrence via limited escalation steps, i.e., signaling for intra-war deterrence.	<u>Goal</u>. U.S. and allied security via deterrence and, if deterrence initially fails, the prevention of escalation by the re-establishment of deterrence via graduated escalation steps; in the event of utter deterrence failure, the limitation of damage to the United States and allies directly, if feasible.
<u>Means</u>. The overwhelming deterrent effect created by secure retaliatory nuclear threats to population and industry. Such threats are easy to establish and maintain because the "crystal ball effect" makes nuclear deterrence uniquely effective. The specific characteristics of the opposing leaderships involved do *not* determine opponents' ultimate cost-benefit calculations in ways that preclude effective easy deterrence.	<u>Means</u>. The deterrent effect on opponents' leaderships created by U.S. strategic forces capable of threatening all types of potential targets—potentially including an opponent's nuclear forces. The "crystal ball effect" helps nuclear deterrence to function, but opposing leaderships' unique cost-benefit calculations can significantly affect the functioning of and requirements for deterrence.
<u>Basis for U.S. Deterrence Credibility</u>. Fear of the "chance" of uncontrolled U.S. nuclear escalation deters: a "threat that leaves something to chance." *Logically* incredible threats can deter.	<u>Basis for U.S. Deterrence Credibility</u>. Opponents' belief that the United States would deliberately initiate nuclear escalation, if necessary, to protect vital interests; U.S. capabilities to protect its population reinforce the credibility of this threat—a threat that leaves little to chance. *Logically* incredible threats may provoke.

---

[191] Figure 2 is adapted from, Payne, *The Great American Gamble*, op. cit., pp. 51-53.

Primary Potential Problem for Effective Deterrence. Reciprocal fears of surprise attack instigated by "destabilizing" strategic offensive/defensive forces that threaten the effectiveness of retaliatory capabilities.	Primary Potential Problem for Effective Deterrence. U.S. vulnerability to nuclear coercion, leading opponents to dismiss the credibility of the U.S. nuclear response to its provocation.
How to Address Challenge to Effective Deterrence. Minimize reciprocal fears by limiting "destabilizing" strategic forces through unilateral and/or cooperative measures. Example: 1972 ABM Treaty essentially precluding effective strategic missile defense.	How to Address Challenge to Effective Deterrence. Make U.S. nuclear threat credible by denying opponents any reasonable expectation that they could deter the United States from nuclear escalation following a severe attack on its vital interests. Some U.S. defense of society can contribute to deterrence credibility.
Prioritization of Deterrence and Damage Limitation. Stable deterrence is a higher priority than the largely ineffective and unreliable damage-limitation potential available via defensive capabilities. Defenses in general are ineffective, unnecessary for deterrence, and likely destabilizing.	Prioritization of Deterrence and Damage Limitation. The goals of deterrence and damage limitation are inseparable because damage limitation can contribute to U.S. deterrence credibility: even imperfect damage-limitation efforts could be valuable for deterrence. And, because war can happen, U.S. society should be protected to the extent possible.
Force Recommendations. Mutual deployment of relatively small, "stabilizing," secure forces for threatening retaliation against population and industry—including limited nuclear escalation options for signaling intrawar deterrence. Mutual avoidance of "destabilizing" offensive or defensive strategic capabilities that could be perceived as undermining the opponent's retaliatory threat.	Force Recommendations. U.S. deployment of the flexible offensive and defensive strategic systems necessary to threaten the spectrum of potential opponents' values for *credible* deterrence purposes and to limit damage to U.S. society to the extent feasible in the event of war.

Competing Deterrence Narratives and the Contemporary Nuclear Debate

It is important to note that for decades the different narratives discussed above and illustrated in Figure 2 have driven much of the interrelated U.S. debate on nuclear deterrence and the value of strategic defense. Because their differing "extra-Realist" elaborations are so contrary, so typically are their conclusions. They establish different and largely incompatible standards for deterrence and different definitions of the types of forces that are said to contribute to or degrade deterrence.

This point is not of historical interest alone; these two deterrence narratives continue to undergird most opposing positions in the contemporary debates about nuclear policy and forces. *Today's competing arguments are largely unintelligible in the absence of an understanding of these divergent narratives* because the contending claims about what is or is not "stabilizing" or required for deterrence tend to be extensions of their different assumptions and projections. An observer cannot know the actual meaning of the competing claims about deterrence requirements and "stability" without a narrative roadmap.

Contemporary positions for or against the Obama and now Trump Administrations' nuclear modernization program tend to follow one narrative or another as the basis for their respective arguments. Largely following the easy deterrence narrative, for example, critics make confident generalized claims about force requirements for deterrence and, in doing so, tend to see *no deterrence need for and considerable potential instability* in much of the Obama and Trump Administrations' comprehensive plan to modernize the U.S. strategic nuclear triad of ICBMs, sea-based strategic ballistic missiles, and strategic bombers.

Several examples illustrate this point—literally hundreds are available:

The United States should adopt a deterrence-only strategy that recognizes neither Russia nor China has strong intrinsic reason to initiate a nuclear attack...and that deterring such attacks can be assured by a relatively small number of survivable U.S. nuclear weapons....The United States could fully support the strategy with a monad composed of nuclear-powered ballistic-missile submarines (SSBN).[192]

Some have argued that a new nuclear-capable air-launch cruise missile is needed to allow future presidents the 'flexibility' to engage Russia or China in limited nuclear war. That is Cold War thinking and it is dangerous.[193]

First and foremost, the United States can safely phase out its land-based intercontinental ballistic missile (ICBM) force, a key facet of Cold War nuclear policy....The submarine force alone is sufficient to deter our enemies and will be for the foreseeable future....But the development of new air-launched nuclear cruise missiles, which has been proposed, is unnecessary and destabilizing. We can maintain an effective bomber force without a nuclear cruise missile.[194]

---

[192] Bruce G. Blair, Jessica Sleight and Emma Claire Foley, *The End of Nuclear Warfighting: Moving to a Deterrence-Only Posture* (Washington, D.C.: Global Zero, September 2018), pp. 6-7.

[193] William Perry and Andy Weber, "Mr. President, Kill the New Cruise Missile," *Washington Post*, October 15, 2015, available at htpps://www.washingtonpost.com/opinions/mr-president-kill-the-new-cruise-missile/2015/10/15/e3e2807c-6ecd-11e5-9bfe-e59f5e244f92_story.html.

[194] William Perry, "Why It's Safe to Scrap America's ICBMs," *The New York Times*, September 10, 2016, available at

And any one of them [ballistic missile carrying submarines] (carrying as many as 192 thermonuclear warheads) is capable of inflicting unacceptable damage on that adversary. Thus our submarines alone give us an assured deterrence.[195]

After all, even a single surviving SSBN could unleash destruction never before seen in human history....A submarine-based monad is more than sufficient for America's deterrence needs.[196]

Each ballistic missile system has multiple types of nuclear warheads, the bomber force carries both gravity bombs and nuclear-armed cruise missiles, and there are more submarines deployed than needed. This belt-and-suspenders approach to nuclear forces may have made sense during the Cold War, but it has become an unneeded luxury.[197]

In contrast to these arguments generally reflecting the easy deterrence narrative against contemporary triad modernization plans, proponents of sustaining the triad largely follow the difficult deterrence narrative's definition of requirements and emphasize the deterrence need for the

---

http://www.nytimes.com/2016/09/30/opinion/why-its-safe-to-scrap-americas-icbms.html?_r=().

[195] William Perry and James Cartwright, "Spending Less on Nuclear Weapons Could Actually Make Us Safer," *Washington Post*, November 16, 2017, available at https://www.washingtonpost.com/opinions/spending-less-on-nuclear-weapons-could-actually-make-us-safer/2017/11/16/396ef()6-ca56-11e7-aa96-54417592ef72_story.html?utm_term=.2fe3b14ea6e7.

[196] Christopher Preble and Matt Fay, "To Save the Submarines, Eliminate ICBMs and Bombers," *Defense One*, October 14, 2013, available at http://www.defenseone.com/ideas/2013/10/save-submarines-eliminate-icbms-and-bombers/71879/.

[197] Collina and Saetren, op. cit.

flexibility and credibility provided by the triad.   Again, several examples illustrate the point; many are available.

- In 2009, the bipartisan Congressional Strategic Posture Commission, led by former Defense Secretaries William Perry and James Schlesinger, included in its final report the recommendation to sustain the full triad because the "flexibility" needed for deterrence is provided by its three different legs.[198]

- The Obama Administration's 2010 *Nuclear Posture Review* concluded that, "Retaining all three Triad legs will best maintain strategic stability at reasonable cost, while hedging against potential technical problems or vulnerabilities."[199]

- In 2016, Assistant Secretary of Defense Scher testified that the Obama Administration's "approach to meeting the range of challenges we now face or might face in the future is to maintain a deterrent that is robust and stable....This remains best served by sustaining the nuclear Triad...with a diverse range of nuclear explosive yields and delivery modes. The Triad and DCA [Dual-Capable Aircraft] provide the credibility, flexibility, and survivability to meet and adapt to

---

[198] William Perry, James Schlesinger, et al., *America's Strategic Posture: The Final Report of the Congressional Commission on the Strategic Posture of the United States* (Washington, D.C.: United States Institute of Peace, 2009), pp. 25-26.

[199] Department of Defense, *Nuclear Posture Review Report* (April 2010), p. 21, available at https://dod.defense.gov/Portals/1/features/defenseReviews/NPR/2 010_Nuclear_Posture_Review_Report.pdf.

the challenges of a dynamic 21st century security environment..."[200]

- Also, in 2016, Secretary of Defense Carter announced that, "we're sustaining deterrence by taking steps to ensure that all three legs of our nuclear triad do not age into obsolescence. This is part of our government's policy." He emphasized that, "how we deter cannot be static. Rather, it must adapt as threats evolve....strong deterrence doesn't lower the threshold for nuclear war. Instead, it raises it."[201]

- In 2017, eight retired four-star Generals and Admirals, all former commanders of U.S. Strategic Command or its predecessor Strategic Air Command under Democratic and Republican presidents, co-authored an article in which they argue strongly in favor of sustaining the triad because: "The combined capabilities of the triad provide the president with the mixture of systems and weapons necessary to hold an adversary's most valuable targets at risk, with the credibility of an assured response if needed....The United States will need a nuclear deterrent for as far into the future as we can see and a triad shaped to 21st century needs is still the most effective means to provide it."[202]

- Finally, the *2018 Nuclear Posture Review* concludes that effective deterrence requires "the

---

[200] Scher, op. cit., p. 3.

[201] Carter, "Remarks by Secretary Carter to Troops at Minot Air Force Base, North Dakota," op. cit.

[202] C. Robert Kehler, et al., "The U.S. Nuclear Triad Needs an Upgrade," *The Wall Street Journal*, January 11, 2017, available at http://www.wsj.com/articles/the-u-s-nuclear-triad-needs-an-upgrade-1484179459.

survivability and flexibility of U.S. nuclear forces
to provide the United States with multiple
options....The increasing need for this diversity
and flexibility, in turn, is one of the primary
reasons why sustaining and replacing the nuclear
triad and non-strategic nuclear capabilities is
necessary.   The multiplicity of platforms,
weapons, and modes of operation inherent in the
triad and U.S. non-strategic nuclear forces,
provide a significant margin of flexibility and
resilience."[203]

The contemporary public debate about U.S. physical
defenses against strategic nuclear attack also follows the
divergent paths charted by the easy and difficult deterrence
narratives. For example, commentary opposed to strategic
missile defense continues to argue that it is too expensive,
ineffective and likely to be "destabilizing."[204] Commentary
in favor, including from the Obama and Trump
Administrations, argues that the capability to defend
against limited nuclear missile threats is important for
deterrence and for the protection of U.S. society against the
types of missile threats posed by rogue states such as North
Korea.[205]   These now-familiar opposing positions
correspond to the competing deterrence narratives and
have endured over decades.

---

[203] *2018 Nuclear Posture Review*, op. cit., pp. 42-43.

[204] See for example, Eric Gomez, "It Can Get You into Trouble, but It
Can't Get You Out," in, Caroline Dorminey and Eric Gomez, *America's
Nuclear Crossroads* (Washington, D.C.: CATO Institute, 2019), pp. 17-28.
See also, Purcell, op. cit.

[205] See for example, *2019 Missile Defense Review*, op. cit., pp. 25-38.

Summary and Conclusions

In conclusion, there are, of course, variations on these two deterrence narratives and their respective requirements for the United States. But caveats and nuance have been subordinated here to their general points and differences to help facilitate an understanding of the distinctions and their implications. The constant push and pull between these two differing basic conceptions of deterrence help greatly to explain the decades-long U.S. nuclear policy debate on the subject, including much of the contemporary policy debate. While starting from a shared Realist orientation, the easy and difficult deterrence narratives include contrary "extra-Realist" expectations about opponent calculations, decision-making and behavior. The easy deterrence narrative posits consistent, predictable caution and sensible calculations. Difficult deterrence posits the potential for great variation, to include reckless behavior and war.

These differences are the dynamics behind their contrary approaches to deterrence and lead logically and directly to their very different definitions of deterrence requirements and the conditions consistent with stability. Their contradictory deterrence force requirements are both logical and coherent given their different starting points. Interestingly, their contrary starting points regarding opponent calculations have historical precedents. Some Soviet and U.S. behavior during the 1962 Cuban Missile Crisis certainly appears to show elements of sensible caution — each side picked its way through the crisis seeking to avoid nuclear war — as is expected by the easy deterrence narrative. Yet, the 1973 Yom Kippur War certainly appears to have included calculations inconsistent with any expectation of sensible, reasonable caution. "Uncertainty" did *not* deter — as the difficult deterrence narrative warns.

Proponents of each narrative often criticize the other for offering mistaken force recommendations. In fact, neither is "mistaken" if judged by its own assumptions and logic. They apply different and largely incompatible measurement standards to answer the question "how much is enough?" and, unsurprisingly, they reach competing conclusions. Easy deterrence force recommendations are wholly inadequate as defined by difficult deterrence measures. In turn, difficult deterrence force requirements include capabilities that are wholly unnecessary and even destabilizing according to easy deterrence standards. Depending on which deterrence narrative is the basis for judging, maintaining the U.S. triad of strategic nuclear forces is either essential for continued deterrence or unnecessary and destabilizing. The preferred narrative virtually determines the judgment.

This is the debate that has carried on for decades and continues today. It is akin to two ship captains charting entirely different courses to the same intended destination, each wondering how the other can be so misguided when the proper course is so obvious. As the U.S. debate about the contemporary nuclear modernization program picks up, any observers who want to understand how seemingly equally-credentialed experts can make diametrically-opposed claims must first understand the competing narratives underlying those opposing claims. They must look behind the curtain because the integrity of the claim depends on the veracity of the narrative.

Chapter 3
Summary and Conclusions:
Three Competing Narratives

Chapters 1 and 2 examined three separate, alternative narratives regarding nuclear weapons, deterrence and disarmament: Idealism, and the easy and difficult deterrence narratives. There is some consensus among the three. Each recognizes the current international system is anarchic to a greater or lesser degree, and the goal of each is to help ensure the absence of nuclear conflict.

However, there are striking differences separating these three narratives: first, Idealists and Realists generally differ over the potential for the transformation of the international system and disarmament; and second, there is sharp disagreement as to whether deterrence is easy and highly reliable or difficult and subject to failure. These three narratives have different expectations about state and leadership behavior in an anarchic international system, and these different expectations lead them to incompatible conclusions regarding the pursuit of their common goal, i.e., precluding nuclear war.

Public debate among these narratives, such as it is, generally focuses on their different conclusions to two questions, i.e., should the United States prioritize nuclear deterrence or disarmament efforts; and, if deterrence, should the United States sustain a modest or robust nuclear arsenal for easy or difficult deterrence, respectively? But the conflicting answers to these questions typically are merely logical extensions of the different starting points of these competing narratives, which generally are *not* the subject of commentary, inspection or introspection. Consequently, the U.S. public debate on these issues often is superficial — focusing on competing conclusions rather than the fundamental differences in the assumptions and logic behind those competing conclusions.

Idealism and Realism: Worlds Apart

The conflicting Idealist and Realist expectations about the potential for the transformation of the international order are long-standing.   Idealists foresee the imperative and potential for the establishment of a much more cooperative global order via states' voluntary, intentional subordination of their national sovereignty to international laws, norms and institutions.   Such a cooperative order could enable global nuclear disarmament which, in turn, would further advance this cooperative transition — possibly to some form of benign and reliable global governance and collective security.   This Idealist foundation often, if not always, is the implicit basis for nuclear disarmament advocacy.

In contrast, Realists generally see such a global transformation as perpetually promised, but never realized. The immediate post-Cold War era seemed to some Realists to offer historically unique possibilities, but traditional patterns of inter-state conflict soon resumed with a vengeance. Reluctantly, most Realists are convinced that the structure of the international system and enduring patterns of human behavior likely preclude international relations from getting to the Idealists' transformed world — at least in any predictable fashion or time frame. Realist assumptions, logic and observations of the world typically do not lead elsewhere. For example, Herman Kahn offered his challenging prescription for nuclear deterrence because he assumed the continued absence of a benign global order: "No sober student of the international scene visualizes anything of this sort!"[1] Given that starting point and his

---

[1] Herman Kahn, *The Nature and Feasibility of War and Deterrence*, P-1888-RC (Santa Monica: RAND Corporation, January 20, 1960), p. 43.

additional expectations regarding the potential behavior of opponents, Kahn logically could not conclude otherwise.

These differing Idealist and Realist expectations about the prospects for transformation typically lead to mutually exclusive conclusions about the potential for nuclear disarmament for the foreseeable future and, correspondingly, to conflicting conclusions about the value and priority of sustaining national nuclear capabilities for deterrence. The Idealist focus on and promotion of global cooperative transformation and nuclear disarmament clearly find greater favor in most popular commentary, academic writings and exhibitions of elite opinion. As Paul Bracken has observed, calling for the elimination of nuclear weapons, "shows that one's heart is in the right place."[2] This favor is reflected in many ways, but perhaps most obviously by the award of the 2017 Nobel Peace Prize to the International Campaign to Abolish Nuclear Weapons and the 2009 Peace Prize to President Obama for his commitment to nuclear disarmament. In addition, every generation of the nuclear age has seen a popular movement, occasionally including some form of mass public demonstration, in support of a ban on or severe limitations on nuclear weapons. One would look in vain for similar displays in support of Realist thought. Lawrence Freedman observes that nuclear deterrence "was never likely to inspire a popular following. Campaigners might march behind banners demanding peace and disarmament...but successful deterrence, marked by nothing much happening, is unlikely to get the pulse racing. It has no natural political constituency."[3]

---

[2] Paul Bracken, "Whatever Happened to Nuclear Abolition?," *The Hill*, March 19, 2019, available at https://thehill.com/opinion/national-security/434723-whatever-happened-to-nuclear-abolition.

[3] Lawrence Freedman, *Deterrence* (Malden, MA: Polity Press, 2004), p. 25.

This apparent appeal of Idealist thought comes as no surprise to Realists who have long recognized that their observations of the world and corresponding recommendations generally lack public appeal, particularly in the United States.[4] The general Realist themes of continuing international conflicts of interest and potential for war, and the associated conclusion that there is an enduring need to arm, potentially including with nuclear weapons, is unlikely to engender much popular enthusiasm in a political culture that understandably shuns the subject and wants definitive answers to problems. In addition, the continuing call for nuclear deterrence as its answer to the threat of nuclear weapons—however sincere and logical, given Realist thought—lends itself to easy and frequent mockery as being inhumane, a vestige of the Cold War, or the crass voice of the "military-industrial complex."

More basically, however, the Realist's description of international relations as a fundamentally amoral, anarchic arena of conflicting interests and power politics, where "the strong do what they can and the weak suffer what they must" offends the powerful legalist, moralist and egalitarian themes in American culture and politics.[5] This Realist description of international relations as essentially lawless, unfair and unequal does not fare well with the typical American extension of legalism, moralism and egalitarianism from the domestic political sphere to the international arena. Realist explanations that such extensions are illogical given the unique and driving

---

[4] See for example, Hans Morgenthau, *Politics Among Nations: The Struggle for Power and Peace*, Third Edition (New York: Alfred A. Knopf, 1962), pp. 36-37; and, John J. Mearsheimer, *The Tragedy of Great Power Politics* (New York: W.W. Norton & Co., 2001), pp. 22-25.

[5] As the great ancient Greek historian and general Thucydides put it starkly in the Melian Dialogue. See Robert B. Strassler, ed., *The Landmark Thucydides: A Comprehensive Guide to the Peloponnesian War* (New York: Touchstone, 1996), p. 352.

demands of an anarchic international system can hardly compete with the Idealist's high-minded and inspirational callings for and descriptions of a more cooperative, benign system.[6]

Worse yet, Realist skepticism that this unhappy condition can be transformed through the application of reason and enlightened thinking violates the widely preferred belief in the progressive improvement of the human condition. E.H. Carr presented the enduring Realist skepticism that must offend those so convinced of or just hopeful for this progress: "It may turn out to be *untrue* that if men reason rightly about international politics they will also act rightly, or that right reasoning about one's own or one's nation's interests is the road to international paradise." Referring to the many confident Idealist claims of the 1930s, Carr observes trenchantly, "...it should not surprise us that the utopia of the international theorists made so little impression on reality."[7] This is the antithesis to the enlightenment belief in progress based on reason that is so endemic in American values. As Morgenthau concludes in this regard, America's history has created a powerful domestic "belief that involvement in power politics is not inevitable, but only a historic accident, and that nations have a choice between power politics and other kinds of foreign policy not tainted by the desire for power."[8] Realist thought essentially says that there is no such choice in an anarchic system that is likely not open to cooperative transformation via the application of reason. This absence of a cooperative solution built on reason is not preferred by

---

[6] See for example, Colin S. Gray, "Force, Order, and Justice," in, Colin S. Gray, *Strategy and History: Essays on Theory and Practice* (London: Routledge, 2006), p. 170.

[7] Edward Hallett Carr, *The Twenty Years' Crisis: 1919-1939* (New York: Harper and Row, 1964), p. 40. (Emphasis added).

[8] Morgenthau, op. cit., p. 37.

anyone who is sensible, but it stubbornly endures nonetheless.

Despite the much greater appeal of Idealist thought and its accord with American political norms, with few exceptions Realism has dominated U.S. nuclear policy. This is the curious juxtaposition of the much more attractive Idealist vision of international relations and nuclear disarmament and the actual U.S. Realist-oriented policy directions consistently adopted by Democratic and Republican administrations. What accounts for this seeming gulf separating American political culture and actual U.S. policy?

Sir Michael Howard's explanation presented in Chapter 1 deserves repeating: "Nobody who has been brought into contact with that inner group of civil and military specialists who are responsible for the security of this country can fail to notice the almost physical pressure exerted on them by that responsibility, affecting their processes of thought (and often their manner of speech) in much the same way as the movements of a man are affected when he tries to walk in water....they share a common skepticism as to the possibility of disarmament, or indeed of the creation of any effective international authority to whom they can turn over any portion of their responsibilities." He adds, "the impatient onlookers, who have never themselves been plunged into that element, cannot understand why."[9]

Indeed, for many, perhaps most of those government officials responsible for U.S. security who receive daily or periodic briefings/reports on the threatening activities of self-described opponents, the cooperative transformation of the globe, including nuclear disarmament, seems wholly divorced from a plausible, foreseeable future. The distance between the cooperative world order envisaged by Idealists and opponents' frequently threatening actions and rhetoric

---

[9] Michael Howard, *Studies in War and Peace* (New York: Viking Press, 1964), pp. 215-216.

appears insurmountable. The challenge of keeping up with and countering external threats, including nuclear threats, is daunting and draining enough. Perhaps many of those threats will come to naught, but others are or will become real, and to plan otherwise seems a dereliction of reason and responsibility. In such a context, the *realization* of a new cooperative world order, as opposed to *describing* it, seems utterly beyond the art of the possible. A senior NATO official, Michael Rühle, offered an insightful comment in this regard that will ring true for many, perhaps most, who have had some level of national security responsibility: "Decision makers...seek incremental ideas that move things forward and that are, above all, achievable... Decision makers will filter everything they hear through the lens of political or military practicability."[10]

This is not to suggest that officials so burdened with national security responsibilities and information must be correct in their less-than-Idealistic expectations of the future and corresponding policy positions. It is to understand that, as Sir Michael observes, those so exposed will be shaped by the experience in ways that are likely to seem incomprehensible to others who are not.

The point here is that Idealist and Realist narratives ultimately are predicated on divergent speculation about the direction of history. Some insist that the world is in the process of profound progression toward their ideal, and *that this is the contemporary reality*: "...optimism is the most logical, sound, and defensible position to arrive at after a rigorous study of history. We do not live in a perfect world.

---

[10] Michael Rühle, "Red Herring & Black Swan: Ground Control to Ivory Tower," *Berlin Policy Journal* (January-February 2020), at https://berlinpolicyjournal.com/red-herring-black-swan-ground-control-to-ivory-tower/.

But we live in a perfectible one. History shows that, over the long run, we collectively have made progress work."[11]

In contrast, while Realists see constant and obvious change in international relations, they do not see emerging the type of broad and enduring international trust and cooperation needed to alter the fundamentally anarchic nature of the system. For example, as noted in Chapter 1, John Mearsheimer concludes, "It is unlikely that all the great powers will simultaneously undergo an epiphany…";[12] and, "there is little reason to think that change is in the offing."[13]

Realists and Idealists seem to live worlds apart. They emphasize *different developments and patterns of behavior* and from this divergent evidence they base their conflicting expectations for the future — leading to Idealist expectations of the potential for fundamental transformation and Realist expectations of resilient interstate anarchy. The contending Idealist and Realist positions on disarmament obviously concern nuclear weapons, but the deeper divide follows from their very different expectations about the direction of international relations and the potential for fundamental, cooperative change.

If the necessary fundamental transformation is, in fact, implausible given the structure of international relations, the continuing lack of interstate trust, and recurring patterns of human behavior, then the prospects for global nuclear disarmament are equally dim and the value of and need for nuclear deterrence will likely endure for a very long time. In contrast, if the needed fundamental transformation is, in fact, in progress and steadily advancing, then the pursuit of nuclear disarmament as the

---

[11] David Rothkopf, "The Case for Optimism," *Foreign Policy*, No. 221 (Nov.-Dec. 2016), p. 56. (Emphasis added).

[12] John Mearsheimer, "Realists as Idealists," *Security Studies*, Vol. 20, No. 3 (2011), p. 428.

[13] Mearsheimer, *The Tragedy of Great Power Politics*, op. cit., p. 362.

policy priority may be a reasonable and even most prudent course.

When matters of national security are in question, prudence—"the weighing of the consequences of alternative political actions" should be considered the priority consideration.[14] But which narrative, Idealist or Realist, deserves to be deemed the more prudent? The answer depends on whether the Idealist or Realist projections of the future are the basis of judgment. It is self-evident that the Idealist's more cooperative world order *ought* to be the future, but whether it *can be* is not self-evident or in any way certain.

Neither Realists nor Idealists can rightly claim a monopoly on truth regarding their competing speculations about the future course of international relations, or a monopoly on logic and reason. The rationales for their respective policy positions are their own competing and yet-unfulfilled speculations about the future. *If international relations continue to be characterized by mistrust and anarchy*, as expected by most Realists, then their general skepticism regarding a policy of disarmament is not unreasonable. In such an environment, concluding that nuclear weapons have value for national security and should be retained is neither foolish nor immoral: they have provided unique and critical deterrence effects to prevent war and its escalation in the past and it is not unreasonable to expect that they could be needed to do so again in the future. As already noted, however, if fundamental transformation is demonstrably underway, then giving policy priority to disarmament may be most reasonable and prudent.

The sharp differences between Realists and Idealists in this regard present a potentially valuable opportunity to compare openly assumptions, assessments, evidence, and conclusions, i.e., reasonable, transparent engagement and

---

14 Morgenthau, op. cit., p. 10.

dialogue. While this type of engagement should be *de rigueur* for a culture that values the freedom of inquiry and the scientific method, it may be expecting too much given the greater ease of operating within a sympathetic echo chamber.

The Idealist's Burden of Proof

For over a century there have been many confident expressions of the requirement for and coming of cooperative systemic transformation. One need only recall the numerous claims surrounding the League of Nations, the Kellogg-Briand Pact and arms control in the 1930s, the United Nations, and the "new world order" and "nuclear zero" of the post-Cold War era. To date, the many claims of transformation have failed to materialize — each has collapsed in its own time. Most recently, the Nuclear Ban Treaty has not been endorsed by the nuclear powers or the many non-nuclear U.S. allies who benefit from U.S. extended nuclear deterrence — even traditionally anti-nuclear Japan has not endorsed it. Apparently they continue to see nuclear deterrence as important for national security. It is likely relatively easy for nuclear "have not" states to agree that no state should have nuclear weapons — but an imprudent prospect for states that deem nuclear deterrence to be critical to their security.

In the contemporary international security environment the potential for the profound cooperative transformation needed for nuclear disarmament appears particularly remote. U.S., Russian, Chinese, British, French, North Korean and many other leaderships certainly appear to share the perspective that the international order remains dangerous and, correspondingly, that nuclear weapons contribute to their national security goals and aspirations. The United States is concerned with apparent Russian and Chinese expansionism and increasing nuclear capabilities and threats. Russia and China seek to restore or expand their respective "places in the sun," and appear to see nuclear power as valuable in that endeavor—particularly because they each also see the United States and its allies as the primary impediment to their goals. Key U.S. allies in the neighborhoods of these revisionist great powers see themselves at considerable risk.[15] In such a context, as Mearsheimer suggests, the burden of proof is on Idealists to demonstrate that these states and many others are in the process—or surely will be—of the timely and enduring epiphanies needed for systemic transformation and disarmament.

Realists have heard optimistic claims many times; yet transformation seems ever to be on the horizon. Most recently were the immediate post-Cold War Western expectations about a "New World Order" and "nuclear abolition." Those expectations now appear as premature as past expansive Idealist claims. Given the many past premature Idealist claims of transformation, Realists unsurprisingly ask: what are the indicators that now portend a fundamental transformation away from the historic cycles of inter-state self-seeking, conflicting interests and the potential for war? Some suggest that the rise of international and transnational institutions now indicates that fundamental transformation is in process. Yet, there have been many types of international institutions for millennia and it is many of these institutions that have faded rather than the fundamentally anarchic character of international relations. What new ingredients

---

[15] Japanese Defense Minister Taro Kono recently said, "With regard to China, I believe that such Chinese military developments represent a serious concern." See, Taro Kono, "Managing an Increasing Uncertain Security Environment," *Defense News*, December 2, 2019, available at https://www.defensenews.com/outlook/2019/12/02/japan-defense-minister-managing-an-increasingly-uncertain-security-environment/.

are now in play that should be deemed transformative; why and how do we know them?

There is little challenge in *describing*, even in detail, a more cooperative new world order or explaining why such a system could have dramatic advantages over international anarchy. The former has been done repeatedly and the latter is self-evident. Nor is it a challenge to *describe* a step-by-step process that *in theory* could move the international system toward fundamental transformation and disarmament, e.g., resolving regional conflicts, reducing/eliminating the value of nuclear weapons and deterrence, and establishing a trustworthy cooperative/collective means of security and conflict resolution. It surely is logical that disarmament could follow the realization of these steps. But repeatedly making that observation is not very useful. It simply changes the question from how to disarm to how to realize the transition that somehow must come into being. The unmet challenge is in explaining why historically self-interested national leaderships will (as opposed to should) move in this direction, and demonstrating *that the various series of common epiphanies needed to get "from here to there" will occur and endure*.

In short, Idealists need to explain why those charged with national security responsibilities can now reasonably conclude that national self-seeking, mistrust, and historic cycles of conflict and war are fading globally and that the expectation of reliable cooperation and enduring trust is becoming a *prudent basis for national policies*. Demonstrating that the Idealists' envisaged cooperative future is now so likely that it is prudent to begin re-orienting national policies and goals accordingly — despite the risks that such expectations, at best, are once again premature — is no easy burden. Inspirational arguments about the self-evident advantages of transformation and disarmament are unlikely to suffice if evidence of enduring systemic transformation—particularly among opponents—is not also forthcoming.

It should be emphasized that systemic transformation cannot be deemed impossible. As James Goodby rightly observed (quoted in Chapter 1), there is no "law of nature" that precludes the possibility. But there are indeed seemingly enduring factors working against cooperative systemic transformation, with millennia of historical experience illustrating the point. The question posed in Chapter 1 remains: *While leaderships around the world clearly are willing to take risks to expand or protect their national position, power and sovereignty, will they do so consciously, intentionally and repeatedly in ways that diminish their national sovereignty and power, and would likely threaten their national security, if opponents prove not to be similarly and reliably enlightened?* Are factors now favoring transformation truly likely to overcome the powerful structural drivers of system continuity in any predictable, reliable fashion? For example, can the absence of inter-state trust that has been a fundamental cause of conflict and the security dilemma be overcome by enduring mutual trust, including among opponents? Perhaps, but evidence of such a transition is far from obvious; the burden of proof is on Idealists to present it clearly, preferably minus any suggestion of Realist willful ignorance or ill intent.

Easy and Difficult Deterrence Narratives: Worlds Apart

As detailed in Chapter 2, while agreeing on the value of nuclear deterrence—at least for now—two largely contrary deterrence narratives have emerged based on initial Realist assumptions. These are described here as easy deterrence and difficult deterrence; they have been the basis for much of the U.S. nuclear policy debate for decades. Different extra-Realist "add-ons" drive them to conflicting answers to the questions that are fundamental to deterrence considerations: Are opponents likely to be highly variable in their responses to deterrence threats or consistent and highly predictable? Are punitive threats to societal targets likely to serve as the reliable basis for deterrence or may very different types of threats be required to deter on occasion? Are *uncertain* threats adequate to deter or may highly credible threats be necessary on occasion? If more credible threats are needed, how can U.S. threats be made credible? And ultimately, can deterrence be considered predictable, highly reliable and easy or is it subject to inherent uncertainties and difficulties? Divergent answers to these fundamental questions are the basis for different expectations about the functioning of deterrence that, in turn, drive competing definitions of the conditions that constitute "stability," how to measure "how much is enough?" for deterrence, and how to judge the potential value of physical defenses such as ballistic missile defense.

Again, one of these narratives appears to be much more politically acceptable than the other. The easy deterrence narrative has many points of greater appeal to that segment of the public that is attentive to such matters. Perhaps most importantly, it offers a *relatively* confident answer to the fear of nuclear conflict: nuclear deterrence *will* prevent it and large-scale conventional conflict that could escalate to nuclear war. Deterrence is predictably effective against all types of rational or sensible state opponents and its requirements are consistent, easily known, relatively modest, and easily met and sustained. Correspondingly, the costs for this reliable solution to an otherwise severe problem are also relatively modest. The easy deterrence narrative also is elegant in that it simplifies deterrence considerations — understanding the unique character of the opponent and tailoring deterrence accordingly is largely unnecessary. When considered in toto, these claims suggest that easy deterrence is superior even to the Idealist's goal of nuclear disarmament, i.e., the likelihood of nuclear war can be minimized reliably *without the challenge of first transforming the global order to make disarmament possible.* If so, it is hard to overstate the value of easy deterrence.

Compare this comforting narrative to the alternative narrative that deterrence is difficult, requires tailoring to specific opponents, constant effort and spending to sustain and, with that, the prospects for war still cannot be dismissed—leading some to add that physical defenses against an undeterrable attack also are necessary. The difficult deterrence narrative hardly offers a definitive, satisfying or in any way comforting prescription, and it sits atop the harsh Realist perspective about the international system; it seems designed to lack appeal.

In short, the easy deterrence narrative is comforting and convenient in many ways while the difficult deterrence narrative can only be described as discomforting, even jarring. Herman Kahn acknowledged that his difficult deterrence-oriented prescription lacked much popular appeal: "This is a difficult, unpleasant, and emotional subject: the points raised are often irritating or dismaying, and many readers transfer their irritation and dismay to the author."[16] Nevertheless, Kahn insisted that facts and logic did not allow an alternative, more attractive course. When criticized by a congressman during congressional testimony for "putting this cold war logic of nuclear war and overkill for two peoples in such remorseless terms," Kahn replied, "Do you prefer a warm human error, a nice emotional mistake?"[17]

---

[16] Herman Kahn, "The Arms Race and Some of its Hazards," in *Arms Control, Disarmament and National Security*, Donald G. Brennan, ed. (New York: George Braziller, 1961), pp. 89-90.

[17] Herman Kahn, U.S. House of Representatives, Committee on Foreign Affairs, Subcommittee on National Security Policy and Scientific Developments, Hearings, 91st Congress, 1st Session, *Strategy and Science:*

Despite the much greater inherent attractiveness of the easy deterrence narrative, for decades the difficult deterrence narrative has been reflected to a considerable extent in U.S. policy. Actual U.S. policy, on a consistently bipartisan basis, generally has not aligned with either of those narratives that have greater points of public appeal, i.e., Idealism or easy deterrence. The reason for this may follow from the same dynamic: U.S. officials with national security responsibility are understandably cautious when considering foreign threats, particularly nuclear threats, and both Idealist disarmament and easy deterrence plans may appear to them to entail greater risks than the difficult deterrence narrative.

Competing Speculation

Both the easy and difficult deterrence narratives reference historical evidence to buttress their contrary positions. The former points to the absence of great power war since the mid-20th century as evidence of the predictable reliability of deterrence; the latter concurs that deterrence has been extraordinarily beneficial, but also points to various historical case studies in which the axioms of the easy deterrence narrative were violated as evidence that deterrence may not function as it projects. In both cases, their different expectations about the functioning of deterrence are based on their contrasting speculation about the future contexts and types of opponents against which deterrence is expected to operate.

The speculative nature of both narratives rarely is advertised. Is some prospective nuclear capability essential for deterrence and stabilizing, or unnecessary and destabilizing? Those involved in the public debate often

---

Toward a National Security Policy for the 1970's (Washington, D.C.: USGPO, 1969), p. 154.

write or speak as if their particular answer reflects known truths about the future. Advocates and opponents of some specific nuclear system, such as an ICBM or cruise missile, offer contrasting claims that the system in question surely is needed for deterrence or equally certainly is excessive and "destabilizing." But these conflicting claims generally reflect one deterrence narrative or the other as the basis for judgment because the expected context and character of the opponent determine how "stability" is defined and "how much is enough" for deterrence is calculated. Although public debates tend to focus on some specific system, the claims for and against are extensions of the competing underlying deterrence narratives. These are at the heart of competing arguments, but virtually never addressed as such—it is much easier simply to assert 'it's destabilizing' or 'it's essential' as if there is a known, objective basis for making such statements. There is not; there are competing narratives based on differing speculative expectations about the future.

Because it is the *future functioning of deterrence* that is in question, both narratives must be speculative. Neither can claim to "know" as generalizations what specific force posture will be more or less "stable" and most suitable for deterrence in the future because deterrence requirements and effects cannot be separated from the variable details of the future context and opponent in question—which must be a matter of some speculation. Consequently, there is no known, general, fixed formula for effective deterrence or for a stable force posture in the future—no matter how insistent are claims in the nuclear policy debate. As Colin Gray has observed, whether a deterrence strategy "stands a realistic prospect of succeeding in any particular instance is a question that can be answered only with reference to the unique details of the case at hand."[18]

---

[18] Colin S. Gray, *Maintaining Effective Deterrence* (Carlisle, PA: Strategic Studies Institute, U.S. Army War College, August 2003), p. 15. Sir

If the easy deterrence narrative's answers to the key questions about context and opponent are considered the more valid, then the associated easy deterrence force posture may be considered the most reasonable. If the difficult deterrence narrative's answers to these questions are considered the more valid, then its more demanding associated force posture requirements may be deemed the most reasonable. Each narrative is the most reasonable *if judged from the prism of its own respective assumptions and logical framework*. However, each is woefully wrongheaded if judged by the other's: the easy deterrence force requirements are wholly inadequate if judged by the standards of the difficult deterrence narrative; the difficult deterrence requirements, in turn, are excessive and destabilizing if judged by the easy deterrence standards. Both such judgments, however, are largely speculative by definition because they concern the future functioning of deterrence and its requirements—which will be shaped by currently unknown details of context and opponent. Experts of all types can offer confident claims about what force is or is not needed for deterrence, but "there can be no [known] objectively correct answer" because, "None of the candidate answers are testable save by future events."[19]

In short, definitive contemporary claims about what will or will not be required for deterrence, or excessive, should be recognized for what they are—based on the different speculative assumptions about the future context and character of opponents underlying the competing narratives. This speculation cannot be resolved with great confidence by better methodologies or sharper analyses.

Lawrence Freedman later made this same point: deterrence theory "provides little reliable guidance for policy other than to suggest that close attention is paid to the specifics of a situation rather than a reliance on vague generalizations." Lawrence Freedman, op. cit., p. 117.

[19] Colin S. Gray, *Strategy and Defense Planning: Meeting the Challenge of Uncertainty* (London: Oxford University Press, 2014), p. 2.

There simply are too many inherent unknowns regarding the many possible factors that can affect the future functioning of nuclear deterrence and its requirements. As Herman Kahn emphasized, there is a fortunate absence of empirical data regarding the outbreak of nuclear war on which to base confident conclusions about the functioning of nuclear deterrence.[20] As a result, much of the continuing debate about the requirements for deterrence is based largely on competing but rarely disclosed speculation about context and opponents.

Which narrative ultimately is the more accurate depends on which will prove to have captured the character of future contexts and opponents more precisely: Will the potentially diverse opposing leaderships' goals, perceptions, values and modes of decision-making render opponent behavior unpredictable, even seemingly irrational to American observers — thereby making the functioning of deterrence particularly challenging — as is anticipated by the difficult deterrence narrative? Or, as anticipated by the easy deterrence narrative, will the contexts and character of opponents enable societal threats and the uncertainty of their execution to be adequate for deterrence to function predictably and reliably? If so, the easy deterrence force recommendations should correspondingly be adequate and the potentially "destabilizing" effects of physical defenses may indeed be of greater concern than the value of whatever added deterrence credibility and protection they might provide. As noted, however, the answers to these questions about the future cannot be known with precision and confidence in the present given the irreducible uncertainties pertinent to the functioning of deterrence. Looking back from the 22nd century, it may be clear via the unraveling of history that one of these narratives or the other offered a more accurate

---

[20] As discussed in Keith B. Payne, *Deterrence in the Second Nuclear Age* (Lexington, KY: University Press of Kentucky, 1996), p. 7, footnote 7.

basis for deterrence policy in the mid-to-late 21ˢᵗ century, but that simply cannot be known with confidence in the present. When it comes to predicting the future functioning of deterrence against unknown opponents, in unknown contexts, over unknown stakes, we are all amateurs looking at shadows on the wall.

Nevertheless, as Herman Kahn observed, in the absence of the cooperative global transformation enabling disarmament, preparation for deterrence must go forward. Abdicating in frustration because it is impossible to predict with certainty the composition of "stability," the precise requirements for deterrence, or the policy direction that *ensures* the functioning of deterrence, would be to consciously leave all to chance and luck — a notoriously bad strategy. Instead, policy guidance for deterrence must be as informed as possible with full recognition that the unavoidable uncertainties about the future preclude credible claims that one of these narratives or the other must be "objectively correct" while the other must be "wrong."

With this significant caveat about deterrence and nuclear policy, the key question is: Given what reasonably may be anticipated about future contexts and opponents, is it possible to suggest whether the easy or difficult deterrence narrative offers an approach to deterrence policy *that is more prudent*?   As noted, this was Morgenthau's priority consideration on matters critical to national security.[21]

Where is Prudence?

Which deterrence narrative ultimately is the more prudent is the central question given the stakes involved. The answer depends on which seems to be more suitable to deter future war most safely and reliably with the limited

---

[21] Morgenthau, op. cit., p. 10.

information available in the present. No "objectively correct answer" is possible, but informed speculation is possible. For example, it is possible to observe that evidence from history and contemporary studies of cognition suggest strongly that opponents are likely to have a diversity of goals, perceptions, values and modes of decision-making — some known to outsiders, others not. Leaderships have frequently pursued surprising goals and risked national security in ways that observers, including those in the United States, considered highly unlikely and even irrational at the time.[22] The easy deterrence narrative may be correct in its expectation that uncertain punitive nuclear threats can enforce caution in all rational or sensible opponents, and thus have the intended deterrent effect; it is impossible to claim otherwise with certainty. But, the central driving concern of difficult deterrence is reasonable: at least some future opponents' decision-making and behavior may be contrary to easy deterrence expectations — *as has been the case in the past* — and affect the functioning of deterrence in unexpected ways — again, as it has in the past. This expectation is buttressed by the expanding number and diversity of nuclear threats to the United States — including from revisionist, expansionist states, and states with leaderships that are unfamiliar and/or highly-eccentric by familiar Western norms. This dynamic appears to increase the probability that the decision-making of diverse opponents will be varied and shape the functioning of deterrence in surprising directions.

Given the potential stakes at risk, it would seem that the burden of proof is on the easy deterrence narrative to explain why those responsible for U.S. national security should now be confident that contexts and opponents will predictably and reliably fit the comforting profile it posits

---

[22] Described in Keith Payne, *The Fallacies of Cold War Deterrence and a New Direction* (Lexington, KY: University Press of Kentucky, 2001), pp. 1-15.

of opponents who will, when necessary, be deterred by uncertain U.S. societal threats, i.e., easy deterrence. But this explanation must acknowledge that the character, behavior and apparent calculations of some pertinent past leaderships have been well outside that particular profile for a variety of reasons. Why can it now be expected with confidence that the potential variability in opponents' future decision-making will *not* lead them to surprising — even *apparently* irrational — behavior? What new factors in state behavior now point with high confidence to opponents whose decision-making and behavior can be relied upon to prove so predictably sensible and cautious that deterrence can be expected to work easily? Easy deterrence proponents are welcome to present the evidence and logic behind confidence in this expectation. If it is deemed most plausible, the potential implications for U.S. deterrence policy are profound for the prudent characterization of deterrence requirements and also for U.S. considerations of nuclear proliferation.[23]

There is, however, a challenge in doing so. Assurances of predictably sensible opponent behavior seem open to serious question given the reality of eccentric, occasionally reckless behavior of some U.S. opponents, now including those with growing or potential nuclear capabilities, such as North Korea and Iran, and also given the significant role nuclear weapons appear to play in Russia's and China's respective efforts to revise the existing order and recover or expand their "places in the sun." As noted, even during the Cold War, Herman Kahn acknowledged that it would be

---

[23] Waltz expressed a logical, but countercultural conclusion of his expectations, i.e., that nuclear proliferation could entail *positive* results if it expands the regions made reliably stable by mutual deterrence. Kenneth Waltz, "The Spread of Nuclear Weapons: More May be Better," *Adelphi Papers*, Number 171 (London: International Institute for Strategic Studies, 1981), available at https://www.mtholyoke.edu/acad/intrel/waltz1.htm.

"reckless" for an opponent to strike the United States with nuclear weapons, but that it would be, "even more reckless" for the United States to rely on an opponent's extreme "caution and responsibility" for security, à la easy deterrence.[24]

The difficult deterrence-recommended flexible nuclear threat options and planning cannot ensure the functioning of deterrence in every possible contingency — as its proponents fully acknowledge. Nothing can "ensure" deterrence because opponents ultimately decide to be deterred or not. But a broader and more flexible range of threat options may usefully help to expand the parameters for deterrence to apply to opponents who require more/other than an uncertain threat of societal destruction to be deterred. Having a spectrum of deterrence threat options and focusing on threat credibility seem only prudent in the contemporary threat environment given the diversity of opponents and their nuclear threats, the potential variability of their decision-making, and the range of possible deterrence goals.

In addition, it seems imprudent to place so much confidence in the reliable functioning of deterrence that little or no provision is made for physically defending against even the *limited* nuclear attacks that might be mounted or threatened by a North Korea, Iran or other new nuclear powers in the future. Here again, the difficult deterrence narrative seems the more prudent; easy deterrence offers no opportunity for the reduction of damage if deterrence and intra-war deterrence fail — its focus is on societal threats and argues *against* societal defenses. In short, Waltz's easy deterrence-oriented rhetorical question, "Why should anyone want to replace stable deterrence with unstable defense?" now seems easily

---

[24] Kahn, *The Nature and Feasibility of War and Deterrence*, op. cit., p. 30.

answered:[25]   In the contemporary security environment, strategic defense may be wanted *not* to replace deterrence, but to help protect society against limited attacks when the reliable functioning of deterrence is suspect and strategic defenses appear to offer some potential for meaningfully limiting the consequences of deterrence failure.   There certainly is room to debate the prospective threats that fit this category, but some almost certainly do.

It should be emphasized that the prudence of difficult deterrence includes a continuing role for diplomacy — Kahn emphasized the possible value of negotiations and agreements that are in the mutual security interests of the United States and opponents.[26]   The Realist caveat to this point, however, is to recognize that most, perhaps all opponents are likely to pursue diplomacy, including arms control negotiations, to advance their own self-interested strategic goals — not as a selfless act for the greater global good or to advance an easy American concept of nuclear deterrence stability.   Expectations otherwise are likely to be frustrated.   Nevertheless, Kahn recognized the possible value of nuclear diplomacy early in the Cold War:

> ...as technology advances and as weapons become more powerful and more diverse, it is most likely that there will have to be at least implicit agreements on their use, distribution, and character if we are not to run unacceptably high risks of unauthorized or irresponsible behavior. No matter how antagonistic the Soviets feel toward us, they have common interests with us in this field. This does not mean that they will not try to exploit the common danger to obtain unilateral advantages; it simply means that

---

[25] Kenneth Waltz, in Scott Sagan and Kenneth Waltz, *The Spread of Nuclear Weapons: A Debate Renewed* (New York: W.W. Norton and Co., 2003), p. 153.

[26] Kahn, *The Nature and Feasibility of War and Deterrence*, op. cit., p. 43.

there is an important area for bargaining here, one that we must fully exploit.

Kahn went on to note, however, that doing this would require the United States to pursue, "much higher-quality preparations for negotiations than have been customary."[27] Both of these comments appear to remain pertinent six decades after Kahn wrote them.

Conclusion

Of the three narratives examined here, Idealism and easy deterrence have the greater points of appeal: both offer a confident answer to the fear of nuclear war. Their answers are different, of course, but both suggest a near-definitive solution. Idealism presents a cooperative international system and nuclear disarmament. Easy deterrence does not go there given its initial Realist orientation, but it does claim great safety in nuclear deterrence with modest effort.

Idealist claims about a cooperative global transformation and easy deterrence confidence are both predicated on the presumption of diverse national leaderships consistently behaving in similarly prudent and reasonable ways — either to global disarmament or to the reliable, easy functioning of deterrence. Each contends that national security policies can prudently be based on its respective expectations. Interestingly, proponents of each of these narratives have criticized the other for being "utopian" — a descriptor neither narrative appears to appreciate. If, however, the expectation of diverse national leaderships consistently, repeatedly and similarly behaving in a highly prudent and reasonable fashion is "utopian," then the description fits both the Idealist and easy deterrence narratives.

---

[27] Ibid., p. 43.

There is little chance that the difficult deterrence narrative will be described as utopian or appealing. It offers neither a definitive solution to the threat of nuclear use nor ease. It offers no cooperative global transformation and disarmament, nor confidence that deterrence will work easily and predictably across time. Instead, the difficult deterrence narrative confronts a dilemma that Idealism and easy deterrence avoid, i.e., the conclusion that deterrence is necessary because a cooperative global transformation is unlikely but also difficult and fallible because leadership decision-making is variable and unpredictable. This conclusion presents a profound dilemma. In response to this dilemma that deterrence is necessary but challenging and fallible, difficult deterrence offers for the foreseeable future: 1) the tailoring of deterrence to be as effective as possible; 2) diplomacy to ease friction when possible; and, 3) mitigating to the extent possible the consequences if deterrence fails with intra-war deterrence and feasible defensive preparations. This is a troubling prescription in many ways. It includes no promised ease or certain happy ending, but it is critical to recognize if its basic points are deemed the most plausible. If so, this narrative that appears least appealing, nevertheless, is also the most prudent.

Given the speculative character of each of these narratives, there is enormous opportunity for open, honest, even animated discussions of competing assumptions and analyses. Doing so could strengthen U.S. policy, but seems to have been largely absent for decades in the United States. The preference apparently is for the ease of monologues and the comfort of a friendly echo chamber. Let us hope for better because the shared goal of each narrative could not be more consequential: nuclear war must be prevented and national security preserved. We are more likely to succeed reasoning together.

Index

About the Author

Keith Payne is a co-founder of the National Institute for Public Policy, a nonprofit research center located in Fairfax, Virginia and professor emeritus, Missouri State University.

Dr. Payne has served in the Department of Defense as the Deputy Assistant Secretary of Defense for Forces Policy and as a Senior Advisor to the Office of the Secretary of Defense (OSD). He received the Distinguished Public Service Medal and the OSD Award for Outstanding Achievement. In 2005, he was awarded the Vicennial Medal from Georgetown University for his many years on the faculty of the graduate National Security Studies Program.

Dr. Payne also served as a Commissioner on the bipartisan Congressional Commission on the Strategic Posture of the United States, as a member of the Secretary of State's International Security Advisory Board, and as a member of U.S. Strategic Command's Senior Advisory Group. He is an award-winning author, co-author, or editor of over one hundred and fifty published articles and eighteen books and monographs, some of which have been translated into German, Russian, Chinese or Japanese. Dr. Payne's articles have appeared in many major U.S., European and Japanese professional journals and newspapers.

Dr. Payne received an A.B. (honors) in political science from the University of California at Berkeley in 1976, studied in Heidelberg, Germany and, in 1981, received a Ph.D. (with distinction) in international relations from the University of Southern California.

CPSIA information can be obtained
at www.ICGtesting.com
Printed in the USA
FSHW011738270820
73206FS

9 780985 555320